ACTS 1-12:

A Pentecostal Commentary

Dr. Matthew N. O. Sadiku

Order this book online at www.trafford.com
or email orders@trafford.com

Most Trafford titles are also available at major online book retailers.

Print information available on the last page.

ISBN: 978-1-4907-7623-1 (sc)
ISBN: 978-1-4907-7625-5 (hc)
ISBN: 978-1-4907-7624-8 (e)

Library of Congress Control Number: 2016913543

Trafford rev. 08/31/2016

 www.trafford.com
North America & international
toll-free: 1 888 232 4444 (USA & Canada)
fax: 812 355 4082

CONTENTS

To

My dad, Solomon Sadiku Ojogiri

Other books by the author

Secrets of Successful Marriages
How to Discover God's Will for Your Life
Wisdom: Your Key to Success
Choosing the Best: Living for What Really Matters
Matthew 1-15: A Pentecostal Commentary
Matthew 16-28: A Pentecostal Commentary
Mark: A Pentecostal Commentary
Luke 1-11: A Pentecostal Commentary
Luke 12-24: A Pentecostal Commentary
John 1-11: A Pentecostal Commentary
John 12-21: A Pentecostal Commentary
Romans: A Pentecostal Commentary
1 Corinthians: A Pentecostal Commentary
2 Corinthians: A Pentecostal Commentary
Ephesians: A Pentecostal Commentary
Galatians: A Pentecostal Commentary
Philippians and Titus: A Pentecostal Commentary
Colossians and Philemon: A Pentecostal Commentary
1 & 2 Thessalonians: A Pentecostal Commentary
1 & 2 Timothy: A Pentecostal Commentary
Hebrews: A Pentecostal Commentary
James and Jude: A Pentecostal Commentary
1 & 2 Peter: A Pentecostal Commentary
1-3 John: A Pentecostal Commentary
Revelation: A Pentecostal Commentary

PREFACE

Earnest Christians are hungry for information that makes their Bible come alive. The Christian life can be described as getting to know God better each day. Every Christian should regularly—daily ead the Word of God. We should find time for quiet or personal devotions. The reason we have so many "bad" days is that we do not spend time with God. We must spend time with God if we want His blessings on our lives and desire to hear from Him.

For over 20 years I have used commentaries in my devotions. The blessings derived from the commentaries are overwhelming. I am writing this commentary to share some of those blessings and lessons I have learned over the years.

This commentary provides verse-by-verse exposition and application on Acts. It is different from others in two respects. First, it is brief while some commentaries are unnecessarily wordy and verbose. This commentary does not delve into critical and exegetical details. Therefore, the limits of this commentary forbid that we consider all the views concerning any issue, but an attempt will be made to provide a brief, sound, yet scholarly view.

Second, it is Pentecostal in outlook. This implies that we generally adhere to the doctrine of biblical inerrancy and adopt a literalist approach to the interpretation of the Bible. Pentecostal doctrines include speaking in tongues, gifts of the Holy Spirit, signs and wonders, divine inspiration, divine healing, to mention but a few. The early church was basically Pentecostal in nature, i.e. it exercised considerable freedom in using the gifts of the Holy Spirit in her life and worship. Although this book is written from a Pentecostal perspective, I draw ideas from scholars from all denominations and hope that the book serves all Christians.

The task of writing a commentary on a verse is similar to what the Amplified Bible does to the verse. If the verse in a regular version is regarded as 100%, the Amplified Bible typically amplifies it 150%, while the commentary typically amplifies it 500%. Thus, the commentary helps you see the verse clearly.

It is not easy to write a commentary on any book in the Bible. In order to provide a readable text, this commentary is based on the New International Version (NIV) translation. The commentary is for laymen, pastors, teachers, and all students of the Word. It is designed to enrich your quiet time or personal study by making the commentary clear and simple. With your Bible in one hand and this commentary in the other, you will be able to unpack the deep truths of God's Word. It is my prayer that this commentary brings you both delight and insight in understanding the Word of God.

I owe a great deal to many scholars whose commentaries on Acts I have consulted. It is my pleasure and honor to thank Adebowale E. Shadare and Olawale Oredolapo for reviewing the manuscript. I owe special thanks to my wife for her support and prayer.

ABBREVIATIONS

AB	Amplified Bible
cf.	confer, compare
ESV	English Standard Version
ibid.	*ibidem*, in the same place
KJV	King James Version
LXX	Septuagint, the OT in Greek
NASB	New American Standard Bible
NIV	New International Version
NKJV	New King James Version
NLT	New Living Translation
NRSV	New Revised Standard Version
NT	New Testament
OT	Old Testament
RSV	Revised Standard Version
TLB	The Living Bible
v., vs.	verse, verses

INTRODUCTION

The gospel of Luke along with the book of Acts forms a two-volume history. Luke is the only evangelist to write a sequel to his gospel. "Luke and Acts together, make up about a quarter of the NT, which is more than any other author."[1] While Luke's gospel was the account of Jesus' earthy ministry, Acts was the record of Jesus' continued ministry through the instrument of His apostles. For this reason, the book of Acts is also known as the Acts of the Apostles.

The book of Acts should be treated as an inspired history book of the early church. There is no other book in the Bible like it. Its location within the canon of the NT writings is to provide a historical bridge linking the gospels and the epistles. Without Acts, it would be difficult to know where the churches in the epistles came from. So we stand in the author's debt in preserving this information.

Before proceeding further on our journey through this treasured book, we should first consider some preliminary matters—authorship, the date and recipient, and the message—that warrant attention on this book.

Authorship

Although the book of Acts does not mention its author, it is apparent that Acts 1:1 refers to the same Theophilus mentioned in Luke 1:1-4. The church's long-held tradition that Luke, a coworker of Paul, wrote Luke and Acts is unanimous. His name appears only three times in the NT (Colossians 4:14; 2 Timothy 4:11; Philemon 24), all in the Pauline letters. He was a doctor or physician who was beloved by Paul. He traveled with Paul during his last journey as indicated with the "we" passages in Acts 16:10-17; 20:5-21:18; and 27:1-28:16.

Luke was not one of the twelve apostles Jesus initially selected. He was Greek or Gentile (Colossians 4:10-14). He was probably the only non-Jewish author in the NT. He was probably a Gentile Christian from Antioch of Syria. He was well educated and cultured.

Date and Recipient

It is uncertain when Acts was written. Luke and Acts are written to someone called Theophilus (meaning "one who loves God") (Luke 1:3; Acts 1:1), who was possibly a Gentile Christian of some means. Acts continues where the gospel of Luke left off. Paul was imprisoned in Rome in A.D. 61 and was kept in prison for at least two years. Since Luke concludes Acts with Paul's first imprisonment in Rome, the earliest time he could have been written it was A.D. 62.

Message

Acts is evidently a book for the church since it illustrates and teaches concerning the nature, growth, and purpose of the church. It is fair to consider Acts 1:8 as the summary of its content: "You will receive power when the Holy Spirit comes on you; and you will be my witnesses in Jerusalem, and in all Judea and Samaria, and to the ends of the earth."

In Acts, Luke presents a history of the church for its first thirty years. It traces the work of the Holy Spirit through the birth, development, and maturity of the church. It emphasizes the spread of the gospel from Jerusalem to Rome.

Just as in the gospels and epistles, Jesus is clearly central in Acts. Acts is distinctively Pentecostal. Some have regarded the book of Acts as the Acts of the Holy Spirit since He is mentioned more than fifty times in the book. He directed and controlled the operations of the church. He filled and empowered the disciples to continue their Master's work of preaching, teaching, and healing.

NOTES

1. Derek Carlsen, *Faith & Courage: Commentary on Acts* (Arlington Heights, IL: Christian Liberty Press, 2000), p. v.

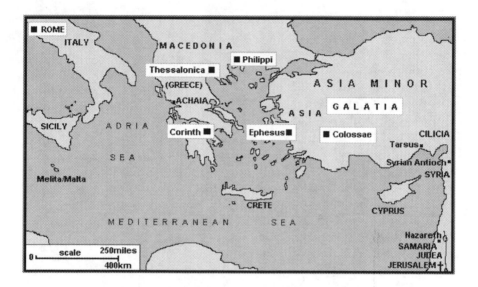

Map of Eastern Mediterranean in the first century A.D.
Source: www.ccel.org

Chapter 1

FORTY DAYS WITH JESUS

Acts 1:1-11

Prologue

Verses 1-3: In my former book, Theophilus, I wrote about all that Jesus began to do and to teach ² until the day he was taken up to heaven, after giving instructions through the Holy Spirit to the apostles he had chosen. ³ After his suffering, he presented himself to them and gave many convincing proofs that he was alive. He appeared to them over a period of forty days and spoke about the kingdom of God.

1 Luke starts with a prologue that links the book of Acts with his former book, the gospel of Luke. He writes both of them to a man called Theophilus. Theophilus means "one who loves God" or "dear to God." He must have been an important person of high rank in government since Luke wrote him two books. Luke is referring Theophilus to the gospel of Luke. There in the gospel, Luke wrote about all that Jesus began to do and to teach. Jesus perfectly lived the truth that He taught. While Christ's redemptive work is finished, its ministerial work is yet to be completed. Acts records the initial stages of that unfinished work of evangelism. It begins where the gospel of Luke left off.

2 "In the first two verses, Luke introduces the main players in the narrative. The three protagonists are Jesus, the Holy Spirit and the apostles."[1] Jesus continued to preach and heal "until the day he was taken up to heaven, after giving instructions through the Holy Spirit

1

to the apostles He had chosen." The day He was taken up to heaven marked the end of Jesus' earthly ministry. During His earthly ministry, He instructed His apostles through the Holy Spirit. The apostles were Christ's commissioned representatives. The Holy Spirit enabled them to obey the Lord's instruction.

3 After His suffering that led to His death on the cross, Jesus presented Himself to them and gave many convincing proofs that He was alive. He entered a room with a locked door and ate with them to show them He was a real person with flesh and bones. He appeared to them over a period of forty days. As a result of these appearances, the apostles became confident that He really did rise from the dead. Why 40 days? As Yon Kwon said, "The number 40 may be symbolic; just as Jesus prepared for his ministry for 40 days (Luke 4:1-2), now his disciples prepare for theirs by being instructed by the risen Jesus for 40 days."[2]

During that time, Jesus spoke mainly about the kingdom of God, the realm where God reigns. The kingdom of God was prophesied by Daniel (2:44; 7:13, 14) and came through Jesus. It was the central message of Christ's teaching during His three-year earthly ministry. The disciples were to seek that kingdom and His righteousness (Matthew 6:33). They were to pray for the kingdom to come (Matthew 6:10). To enter into the kingdom, one must be born again (John 3:3).

The Promise of the Father

Verses 4,5: On one occasion, while he was eating with them, he gave them this command: "Do not leave Jerusalem, but wait for the gift my Father promised, which you have heard me speak about. [5] *For John baptized with water, but in a few days you will be baptized with the Holy Spirit."*

4 Having witnessed Jesus' appearances after His resurrection, it is easy for the apostles to feel they were ready to preach the gospel in their own strength. Jesus dissuaded them to do so. On one occasion, while He was eating with them, He gave them this command: "Do not leave Jerusalem, but wait for the gift my Father promised, which you have heard me speak about." It was imperative for them to stay in Jerusalem until they were "clothed with power from on high." Jesus had repeatedly talked about this (e.g. Luke 11:13; 24:49). Why Jerusalem? Some suggest that this is perhaps a fulfillment of Isaiah 2:3.

5 The word "baptize" means to dip or immerse. John the Baptist performed the baptism of repentance. He even testified that Jesus was the One who would baptize with the Holy Spirit (John 1:33). Jesus said, "For John baptized with water, but in a few days you will be baptized with the Holy Spirit." Before His suffering, Jesus promised His disciples the gift of the Holy Spirit (John 14:16-21; 15:26; 16:7). That Holy Spirit came on Pentecost, exactly ten days after His ascension. They needed the Holy Spirit to energize, enlighten, and encourage them. He was to be the Helper they needed to fulfill the Great Commission.

The Commission

Verses 6-8: Then they gathered around him and asked him, "Lord, are you at this time going to restore the kingdom to Israel?" ⁷ He said to them: "It is not for you to know the times or dates the Father has set by his own authority. ⁸ But you will receive power when the Holy Spirit comes on you; and you will be my witnesses in Jerusalem, and in all Judea and Samaria, and to the ends of the earth."

6 Since Jesus had been talking about the kingdom before and after His resurrection, it only seemed logical for the disciples to ask Him about the restoration of the kingdom. They gathered around Him and asked Him, "Lord, are you at this time going to restore the kingdom to Israel?" They were curious to know Jesus' timetable for the end-times events. They still looked for a political kingdom. Their question was not answered.

7 He said to them: "It is not for you to know the times or dates the Father has set by his own authority." They should not be preoccupied with speculating the time for the coming of the kingdom. They did not need to know the precise time God would establish His kingdom. It was not their business or privilege to know such things. Knowing times and seasons remains one of the secret things that belong exclusively to the Lord (Deuteronomy 29:29).

8 This is the key verse in Acts: "But you will receive power when the Holy Spirit comes on you; and you will be my witnesses in Jerusalem, and in all Judea and Samaria, and to the ends of the earth." "Power" means the ability to do something. Very soon they would receive the power (*dunamis*, Greek) needed for the ministry after the Holy Spirit indwells them. All believers in Christ have in them that spiritual dynamite to enable them witness and serve. Believers "*are* witnesses, and the only question is how effective their witness is."[3]

Their witnessing for the Lord must start from Jerusalem, the city of the Great King (Psalm 48:2). They were to carry out the Lord's mandate there. Then their witness should spread to all other towns in Judea. They should go into the neighboring area of Samaria. Even the despised Samaritans were to become part of the kingdom. Finally, they were to take the gospel to the remotest part of the earth. Here is the Lord's master plan for world evangelization. "Chapter 1-7 tells of the witness 'in Jerusalem,' chapters 8-11 the witness 'in all Judea and Samaria,' and chapters 12-28 the witness 'to the end of the earth.'"[4] As the gospel message spreads, Satan's territory shrinks steadily.

The Ascension

Verses 9-11: After he said this, he was taken up before their very eyes, and a cloud hid him from their sight. [10] They were looking intently up into the sky as he was going, when suddenly two men dressed in white stood beside them. [11] "Men of Galilee," they said, "why do you stand here looking into the sky? This same Jesus, who has been taken from you into heaven, will come back in the same way you have seen him go into heaven."

9 After Jesus gave the important command about the Holy Spirit, He was taken up before their very eyes, and a cloud hid Him from their sight. To their amazement, Jesus was levitated up in the sky. He didn't just disappear, but He was slowly lifted up before their eyes. Thus none of them could doubt where He had gone. Jesus departed this world to return to His former glory. The ascension is associated with Christ's exaltation to sit at the right hand of God in heaven (Ephesians 1:20,21; Hebrews 1:3).

10 They were looking intently up into the sky as Jesus was levitated. Their attention was riveted to the sky. "It was the end of an era. That which had begun in a cradle now ended in a cloud. God in Christ had come down to earth; now He had gone back to heaven."[5]

The upward gaze was interrupted by two men dressed in white clothes, standing beside the disciples. The fact that their clothes were white suggests that the two men were angels sent to address them. The fact that they were two is to establish their credibility as witnesses (Deuteronomy 19:15). Angels are ministering messengers of God. "Angels had announced His birth, angels had watched His temptation, angels had strengthened Him in Gethsemane, angels had heralded His resurrection, and now angels had come to escort Him to the skies."[6]

11 "Men of Galilee," they said, "why do you stand here looking into the sky? This same Jesus, who has been taken from you into heaven, will come back in the same way you have seen him go into heaven." All the apostles were Galileans now; all of them except Judas Iscariot had been Galileans. The angels rebuked the disciples for gazing into the sky instead of obeying Jesus' commands. They assured them that Jesus would return. He will come back in His glorified body, in the clouds, just as He departed.

NOTES

1. Steven Ger, *The Book of Acts: Witnesses to the World* (Chattanooga, TN: AMG Publishers, 2004), p. 18.
2. Yon Gyong Kwon (ed.), *A commentary on Acts* (Minneapolis, MN: Fortress Press, 2015), p. 7.
3. John MacArthur, *The MacArthur New Testament Commentary: Acts 1-12* (Chicago, IL: Moody Publishers, 1994), p. 21.
4. R. Kent Hughes, *Acts: The Church Afire* (Wheaton, IL: Crossway,1996), p. 15.
5. John Phillips, *Exploring Acts* (Grand Rapids, MI: Kregel Publications, 1986), p. 23.
6. Ibid., p. 23.

Chapter 2

MATTHIAS REPLACES JUDAS

Acts 1:12-26

Return to Jerusalem

Verses 12-14: Then the apostles returned to Jerusalem from the hill called the Mount of Olives, a Sabbath day's walk from the city. ¹³ When they arrived, they went upstairs to the room where they were staying. Those present were Peter, John, James and Andrew; Philip and Thomas, Bartholomew and Matthew; James son of Alphaeus and Simon the Zealot, and Judas son of James. ¹⁴ They all joined together constantly in prayer, along with the women and Mary the mother of Jesus, and with his brothers.

12 Jesus had instructed the disciples to go back to Jerusalem and tarry for the Holy Spirit, who would empower them for the task ahead. In obedience to that instruction, the apostles returned to Jerusalem from the hill called the Mount of Olives. That was a Sabbath day's walk from the city. A Sabbath day's walk was the maximum distance one was allowed to travel on the Sabbath and it was about 2,000 cubits or 3,666 feet. It was a short distance.

13 When they arrived, they went upstairs to the room where they were staying. This was probably the place where the apostles ate the Passover meal with the Lord (Luke 22:12). This would give them privacy and would be appropriate for group prayer. Those present in the Upper Room included the remaining eleven apostles. The NT contains four lists of the apostles: Matthew 10:2-4; Mark 3:16-19; Luke 6:13-16; and Acts 1:13.

The minor variations in the lists show that the order was not set in stone. These are the names of the eleven apostles:

- *Simon:* He was also called Peter. Simon is probably a contraction of Simeon, which means "hearing." Jesus changed his name from Simon to Peter, which is a Greek name that means "rock." Peter is the leader of the Twelve and their spokesman. He was fisherman and a native of Bethsaida. He was married (Matthew 8:14) and wrote two epistles.
- *John:* This was the brother of James. He with James and Peter formed an inner circle within the Twelve. He wrote one of the Gospels, three epistles, and the book of Revelation. He was banished to the small island of Patmos and was the last apostle to die.
- *James:* This was the son of Zebedee. He was hot-tempered and was the senior brother of John. To James and John, Jesus gave the name Boarnerges, which means "sons of thunder." He was arrested and executed by Herod. He was the first apostle to die.
- *Andrew:* This was Peter's brother. His name means "manly." He was also a fisherman from Bethsaida. He was a former follower of John the Baptist. He left John the Baptist and followed Jesus. He introduced his brother Peter to Jesus (John 1:35-42).
- *Philip:* His Greek name Philip means "lover of horses." He grew up in Bethsaida, like Peter and Andrew. He too left John the Baptist to follow Jesus. He was the fourth disciple Jesus called (John 1:43) and brought Nathanael (Bartholomew) to Christ.
- *Thomas:* His name means "a twin." He is often known as the "doubting Thomas" because he did not believe the report that Jesus appeared to the disciples during his absence.
- *Bartholomew:* His name means "son of Tolmai." He was also called Nathanael. He was from Cana of Galilee and was a friend of Philip, who led him to Christ.
- *Matthew:* His name means "the gift of God." He is also known as Levi (Mark 2:14). He was formerly a tax collector. He is one of the best known apostles because he wrote the first gospel.
- *James:* This was son of Alphaeus, to distinguish him from James the son of Zebedee. He is called James the less. He might be

a brother of Matthew because Matthew's father was Alphaeus (Mark 2:14)

- *Simon:* He was called the Zealot or the activist, indicating his zeal for God and the Jewish nation. He might have been a former member of the radical Zealot party. He should not be confused with Simon Peter.
- *Judas:* He was the son of James, to distinguish him from Judas Iscariot. He was the brother of James the less. He is also called Thaddaeus (Matthew 10:3), which means "beloved" or "bighearted."

14 The apostles were all joined together constantly in prayer, along with some women who had followed Jesus and Mary the mother of Jesus, and with his brothers. The women apparently included Mary Magdalene, Mary the wife of Clopas, Salome, the mother of Jesus (her only appearance in Acts), and the wives of the apostles. Jesus' biological siblings—James, Joses, Judas, and Simon (Mark 6:3)—were also present. They did not believe prior to the resurrection.

"Prayer begins to appear as a mark of the early church. When they were fearful, they prayed. When they were confused, they prayed. When they were waiting for God to fulfill his promise to them, they prayed. When they needed answer to a question (such as who was to be the twelfth apostle), they prayed."[1] This company of 120 disciples (v. 15) not only prayed, they waited patiently for the Holy Spirit for ten days, the period between the ascension and the day of Pentecost.

The Sin of Judas Reviewed

Verses 15-20: In those days Peter stood up among the believers (a group numbering about a hundred and twenty) [16] *and said, "Brothers and sisters, the Scripture had to be fulfilled in which the Holy Spirit spoke long ago through David concerning Judas, who served as guide for those who arrested Jesus.* [17] *He was one of our number and shared in our ministry."* [18] *(With the payment he received for his wickedness, Judas bought a field; there he fell headlong, his body burst open and all his intestines spilled out.* [19] *Everyone in Jerusalem heard about this, so they called that field in their language Akeldama, that is, Field of Blood.)* [20] *"For," said Peter, "it is written in the*

*Book of Psalms: "'May his place be deserted; let there be no one to dwell in it,'
and, "'May another take his place of leadership.'*

15 During those ten days of waiting, Peter took the lead. Although he
had denied the Lord, Peter had been forgiven by the risen Lord and
restored (John 21:15-18). Peter stood up among the believers (a group
numbering about 120). Some pastors would be discouraged to have just
120 members in their church. But the church of God had to start small,
as illustrated in the parable of the mustard seed.

16 Peter said, "Brothers and sisters, the Scripture had to be fulfilled in
which the Holy Spirit spoke long ago through David concerning Judas,
who served as guide for those who arrested Jesus." He saw Judas' betrayal
as a fulfillment of God's purpose (Psalm 69:25; 109:8). But Judas was
responsible and had no excuse. Nevertheless, his betrayal must not
continue to linger in the back of their minds. They must do something
about it.

17 "He was one of our number and shared in our ministry." Peter was
not ashamed that Judas was one of them. Judas was one of the twelve
apostles Jesus prayerfully selected (Luke 6:12-16). He was placed among
the Twelve because it was necessary for him to betray Christ. He had
preached the gospel, healed the sick, cast out demons, seen the Lord's
countless miracles, and ate with the Lord.

18 Verses 18 and 19 are in parenthesis because they were not part of
Peter's speech and were inserted by Luke for clarification. Judas betrayed
his Master for thirty silver coins. With the payment he received for
his wickedness, Judas bought a field. He was unrepentant and finally
committed suicide. He hanged himself, but the rope snapped. The man
fell headlong, his body burst open and all his intestines spilled out.

19 Everyone in Jerusalem heard about what Judas did, just as the
circumstances surrounding Jesus' death were common knowledge. They
called that field in their Aramaic language *Akeldama* (that is, "Field of
Blood"). Many have identified Akeldama with a cemetery about a half-
mile from Jerusalem. Different theories developed about how the field got
its name.

20 "For," said Peter, "it is written in the Book of Psalms: 'May his place be deserted; let there be no one to dwell in it,' and, 'May another take his place of leadership.'" These two quotations are taken from Psalm 69:25 and Psalm 109:8. As Peter reflected on Scripture, he felt that something must be done to replace Judas, the missing member of the apostles. Thus Peter's application of the Psalms formed the basis of the first important decision the disciples would make—replacing Judas.

The Selection of Matthias

Verses 21-26: Therefore it is necessary to choose one of the men who have been with us the whole time the Lord Jesus was living among us, ²² beginning from John's baptism to the time when Jesus was taken up from us. For one of these must become a witness with us of his resurrection." ²³ So they nominated two men: Joseph called Barsabbas (also known as Justus) and Matthias. ²⁴ Then they prayed, "Lord, you know everyone's heart. Show us which of these two you have chosen ²⁵ to take over this apostolic ministry, which Judas left to go where he belongs." ²⁶ Then they cast lots, and the lot fell to Matthias; so he was added to the eleven apostles.

21 In verses 21 and 22, Peter specified two criteria that they should consider in nominating the person to replace Judas. First, it is necessary to choose one of the men who have been with them the whole time the Lord Jesus was living among them. Such eyewitness involvement was needed for one bearing witness to Jesus. The successor must be an associate of Jesus and one of His original followers. Later apostles such as Paul and Barnabas did not meet this qualification.

22 Peter further clarified that period: beginning from John's baptism to the time when Jesus was taken up from us. Second, he must become a witness with us of His resurrection. Simply put, the person must have been with them from the beginning and must witness Jesus' resurrection. Some argue Paul was the Lord's choice for the twelfth apostle. But Paul did not meet the two criteria. The Lord would definitely not have allowed the eleven apostles to choose the wrong man.

23 So they nominated two men: Joseph called Barsabbas (also known as Justus, his Roman name) and Matthias. Barsabbas means in Aramaic "son of the Sabbath," while Matthias means "gift of God." Although we do not know much about these men, they met the two criteria. They had been with the disciples since the beginning of Jesus ministry and they witnessed His resurrection. They were equally qualified. It would require the Lord to discern which one was rightly selected.

24,25 They involved the Lord in the selection process. They prayed, "Lord, you know everyone's heart. Show us which of these two you have chosen to take over this apostolic ministry, which Judas left to go where he belongs." As they prayed their first recorded prayer, they remembered God's omniscience and His willingness to guide their selection. They were open to whichever candidate God would choose to replace Judas, who fell by transgression and had gone to his own place.

26 Then they cast lots, an OT way of determining God's will. Proverbs 16:33 says, "The Lot is cast into the lap, but its every decision is from the LORD;" while Proverbs 18:18 says, "Casting the lot settles disputes, and keeps strong opponents apart." After casting the lot, it fell to Matthias; so he was added to the eleven apostles. The number twelve was now complete. Some argue that there is no mention about Matthias in the NT. The same could be said of other apostles besides Peter, James, and John.

Right now, the disciples were powerless to impact the world for Christ. They must wait for the Holy Spirit to come.

NOTES

1. B. Bruce Barton et al., *Life Application Bible Commentary: Acts* (Carol Stream, IL: Tyndale House Publishers, 1999), p. 15.

Chapter 3

EXPLOSION AT PENTECOST

Acts 2:1-13

The Coming of the Spirit

Verses 1-4: When the day of Pentecost came, they were all together in one place. ² Suddenly a sound like the blowing of a violent wind came from heaven and filled the whole house where they were sitting. ³ They saw what seemed to be tongues of fire that separated and came to rest on each of them. ⁴ All of them were filled with the Holy Spirit and began to speak in other tongues as the Spirit enabled them.

1 The arrival of the Holy Spirit marked the beginning of the church age. It was a dramatic event. When the day of Pentecost came, the 120 disciples were all together in one place. "Pentecost" is a Greek word which means "fiftieth." It was called the Feast of Weeks in the OT (Exodus 34:22,23) and was celebrated fifty days after Passover (Leviticus 23:15,16). The Holy Spirit came ten days after the Ascension or fifty days after the Resurrection.

2 Suddenly, without warning, a sound like the blowing of a violent wind or a tornado came from heaven and filled the whole house where the disciples were sitting. It was not just wind but a sound like wind, symbolic of the Spirit of God. Like the wind, the Spirit cannot be seen, though His effects can be felt (John 3:8). No one expected the spiritual explosion that came with the Spirit. The outpouring of the Holy Spirit was spectacular and without parallel.

3 First was the hearing, then the sight. The audible sign was followed by the visible one. They saw what seemed to be tongues of fire that separated and came to rest on each of them. What seemed like tongues of fire distributed itself uniformly on the disciples. Like the wind, the fire was another symbol of the Spirit. Fire was a symbol of God's presence in the OT (e.g Exodus 3:2-4; 24:17; 1 Kings 18:38; 2 Kings 2:11). The outpouring of the Spirit fulfilled the prophecy by John the Baptist that Jesus would baptize with the Spirit and fire (Luke 3:16).

4 As a result, all of them were filled with the Holy Spirit. They began to speak in other tongues as the Spirit enabled them. "Other tongues" is from the Greek word *glossolalia*. This depicts believers speaking in human languages previously unknown to them.

There is a difference between being baptized with the Spirit and being filled with the Spirit. One is baptized with the Spirit when one trusts in Jesus for salvation. It is an act of Christ through which He places a believer in His body. It is not a repeated act. Being filled with the Spirit is a continuous experience (Ephesians 5:18). Our realization of being filled with the Spirit depends on our cooperation with the Holy Spirit. One can receive a fresh filling for a specific task.

The ability to speak in tongues is associated with being filled with the Holy Spirit. Some claim that this ability ended with the passing of the apostles and that the gift of tongues was a temporary and transitional gift. There is no biblical support for this. We are still in the church age and speaking in tongues is one the gifts of the Holy Spirit that the church is supposed to enjoy (1 Corinthians 12).

Results of the Spirit's Coming

Verses 5-11: Now there were staying in Jerusalem God-fearing Jews from every nation under heaven. ⁶ When they heard this sound, a crowd came together in bewilderment, because each one heard their own language being spoken. ⁷ Utterly amazed, they asked: "Aren't all these who are speaking Galileans? ⁸ Then how is it that each of us hears them in our native language? ⁹ Parthians, Medes and Elamites; residents of Mesopotamia, Judea and Cappadocia, Pontus and Asia, ¹⁰ Phrygia and Pamphylia, Egypt and the parts of Libya near Cyrene; visitors from Rome ¹¹ (both Jews and converts to

Judaism); Cretans and Arabs—we hear them declaring the wonders of God in our own tongues!"

5 Now there were staying in Jerusalem God-fearing Jews from every nation under heaven. They were Jews and converts to Judaism (v.11), who came from all over the world to celebrate Pentecost. Pentecost was one of the three major feasts Jews were expected to celebrate in Jerusalem—the Feast of Passover, the Feast of Tabernacles, and the Feast of Pentecost.

6 When they heard this sound, a crowd came together in bewilderment, because each one heard their own language being spoken. The supernatural phenomenon attracted the attention of the pilgrims. As John MacArthur said, "The evidence of the Spirit's coming was unmistakable. He manifested His presence to the ears, eyes, and mouths of the believers. But it didn't stop there. His coming had a profound effect on the people of Jerusalem as well."[1]

7,8 Utterly amazed, the crowd asked: "Aren't all these who are speaking Galileans? Then how is it that each of us hears them in our native language?" The disciples, majority of who were Galileans, were not just speaking in tongues; they were speaking the native languages of the crowd so that the crowd could understand what the disciples were saying in tongues.

9-11 The gospel was meant for the whole world and God made provision for it to reach every where. The disciples were speaking in the following 15 languages or nations:

- *Parthians:* They lived in modern Iran.
- *Medes:* They lived in the Parthian empire.
- *Elamites:* They lived in southwestern Iran
- *Residents of Mesopotamia:* They lived between the Euphrates and Tigris.
- *Judea:* This included Palestine and Syria.
- *Cappadocia:* This belonged to the southern part of Asia Minor or modern Turkey.
- *Pontus:* This was a Roman province in northern Asia Minor.

- *Asia:* This was a Roman province comprising west of Asia Minor. It does not refer to the continent of Asia.
- *Phrygia:* This was an ethnic district, consisting of part of Galatia and part of the province of Asia.
- *Pamphylia:* This was a Roman province situated on the south of Asia Minor.
- *Egypt:* This belonged to northern Africa.
- *The parts of Libya near Cyrene:* This was northwestern Africa along the Mediterranean Sea.
- *Visitors from Rome:* This was the city of Rome across the Mediteranean.
- *Cretans:* These were from the island of Crete in southern Greece.
- *Arabs:* These were from the Nabatean Arabic kingdom.

This implies that the disciples were speaking in fifteen different languages and possibly more. The crowd heard them declaring the wonders of God in their own tongues! Nothing could show more clearly than the multi-lingual, multi-national, multi-racial nature of the kingdom of God. Through this manifestation of the Spirit and the international nature of the crowd, God prepared the means of spreading the gospel worldwide. He also reversed the curse that had occurred at the towel of Babel, where there was a loss of communication (Genesis 11:1-9). God's judgment at Babel scattered the people because He confused their language, but His blessing at Pentecost united people.

Reactions of the Crowd

Verses 12,13: Amazed and perplexed, they asked one another, "What does this mean?" ¹³ Some, however, made fun of them and said, "They have had too much wine."

12 As is always the case when truth confronts a group of people, some will accept it, and some will reject it and mock at it. Positive reaction with awe was appropriate. Amazed and perplexed, the bystanders asked one another, "What does this mean?" What was the commotion all about? Their legitimate question would be answered by Peter very soon.

13 However, some bystanders already formed negative opinions. They made fun of the disciples and said, "They have had too much wine." They mocked them saying, "The ignorant and uneducated Galileans must be drunk." They mocked and rejected the idea that this was a work of God. As John Phillips said, "The world has always had its mockers. Men mock at sin, they mocked at the Savior, they mock the saints."[2] Modern men commit the error of attributing the supernatural to natural causes.

NOTES

1. John MacArthur, *The MacArthur New Testament Commentary: Acts 1-12* (Chicago, IL: Moody Publishers, 1994), p. 43.
2. John Phillips, *Exploring Acts* (Grand Rapids, MI: Kregel Publications, 1986), p. 46.

Chapter 4

PETER'S SERMON – PART 1

Acts 2:14-36

The Refutation

Verses 14,15: Then Peter stood up with the Eleven, raised his voice and addressed the crowd: "Fellow Jews and all of you who live in Jerusalem, let me explain this to you; listen carefully to what I say. ¹⁵ These people are not drunk, as you suppose. It's only nine in the morning!

14 To explain what is happening, Peter stood up with the other eleven apostles. He had to raise his voice to address a huge crowd because there was no public address system back then. He addressed the crowd: "Fellow Jews and all of you who live in Jerusalem, let me explain this to you; listen carefully to what I say." Peter's first sermon was great because it was simple, relevant, Scriptural, and Christ-centered.

15 Peter refuted and dismissed the false accusation that the disciples were drunk. "These people are not drunk, as you suppose. It's only nine in the morning!" It was only 9 am and people did not get drunk so early. Peter explained the absurdity of that accusation. He made his message relevant to the questions that were on the minds of the people.

The Explanation

Verses 16-21: No, this is what was spoken by the prophet Joel:

[17] "'In the last days, God says,
I will pour out my Spirit on all people.
Your sons and daughters will prophesy,
your young men will see visions,
your old men will dream dreams.
[18] Even on my servants, both men and women,
I will pour out my Spirit in those days,
and they will prophesy.
[19] I will show wonders in the heavens above
and signs on the earth below,
blood and fire and billows of smoke.
[20] The sun will be turned to darkness
and the moon to blood
before the coming of the great and glorious day of the Lord.
[21] And everyone who calls
on the name of the Lord will be saved.'

16 Rather than being drunk, what had happened was the extraordinary phenomenon of believers who were Spirit-filled. That was in fulfillment of what was spoken by the prophet Joel (Joel 2:28-32). This was a bold assertion. Quoting the Scriptures buttressed Peter's words with divine authority. It is vital to give the people a scriptural reference for what they were observing as Peter did.

17 The prophet Joel prophesied, "'In the last days, God says, I will pour out my Spirit on all people. Your sons and daughters will prophesy, your young men will see visions, your old men will dream dreams." The "last days" include days between the first and second comings of Jesus. Before this occasion, the Holy Spirit was only given to judges, kings, priests, and prophets for service. Only now would the Spirit be poured on all people who called on the name of the Lord irrespective of their status. What had been rare and restricted was now made available to all believers. Their sons and daughters will act like prophets, foretelling the future. Young men will see visions as God would reveal Himself. Old men will dream dreams as the product of God's work. Prophecy, visions, and dreams are supernatural ways God reveals Himself to His people.

18 The Holy Spirit was poured out for the humanity—to men, women, sons and daughters, slaves, Jews and Gentiles. "Even on my servants, both men and women, I will pour out my Spirit in those days, and they will prophesy." God intends both men and women to serve Him. He will pour out His Spirit on them and they will prophesy.

This is what distinguishes Christianity from other religions. In other religions, people serve God in their strength. In Christianity, people serve God in the power of the Holy Spirit. This makes a huge difference.

19 "I will show wonders in the heavens above and signs on the earth below, blood and fire and billows of smoke." The events described here did not occur at Pentecost. These heavenly wonders were not supposed to be part of the Pentecostal happening. They are associated with the days before the second coming of Christ. This indicates that Joel's prophecy was only partially fulfilled at Pentecost. Peter was looking forward to signs and wonders that would announce the second coming of the Lord.

20 Peter continues his quotation from Joel: "The sun will be turned to darkness and the moon to blood before the coming of the great and glorious day of the Lord." These events will happen "afterward." They will occur before the great day of the Lord (Isaiah 13:10; Matthew 24:29,30). The outpouring and prophesying would continue until these signs are fulfilled at the end of the age.

21 This verse gives the reason for the outpouring of the Holy Spirit. The Holy Spirit convicts of sin and the need for salvation. "And everyone who calls on the name of the Lord will be saved." Salvation is available to everyone who calls on the name of the Lord. "Salvation is found in no one else, for there is no other name under heaven given to men by which we must be saved" (Acts 4:12). Jesus is the only name God exclusively honors for salvation.

The Life and Death of Christ

Verses 22,23: "Fellow Israelites, listen to this: Jesus of Nazareth was a man accredited by God to you by miracles, wonders and signs, which God did among you through him, as you yourselves know. ²³ This man was handed over to you by God's deliberate plan and foreknowledge; and you, with the help of wicked men; put him to death by nailing him to the cross.

22 Peter challenged his fellow Israelites to listen carefully. He told them about Jesus of Nazareth, who was a man accredited by God to you by miracles, wonders and signs. God did all this among them through Jesus, as they fully knew. The Jews already knew of it; they had seen Jesus' work and had rejected Him.

Christ is referred to as Jesus of Nazareth because it identified Him with His hometown. "This name for our Lord reflects His wonderful condescension in leaving the glory of heaven to live in a humble Galilean village."[1]

23 This Man was handed over to them by God's deliberate plan and foreknowledge. By God's design, Jesus was delivered up to His enemies so that He might become the Savior of the world. He was betrayed by Judas. The religious leaders, with the help of wicked men put Him to death by nailing Him to the cross. Peter did not hesitate to tell them that they were responsible for the death of Christ on the cross. This was all planned and ordained by God. Jesus was the Lamb of God slain from the foundation of the world (Revelation 13:8). Jesus Himself said, "No one takes it from me, but I lay it down of my own accord" (John 10:18).

The Resurrection of Christ

Verses 24-32: But God raised him from the dead, freeing him from the agony of death, because it was impossible for death to keep its hold on him. ²⁵ David said about him:

"'I saw the Lord always before me.
Because he is at my right hand,
I will not be shaken.
²⁶ Therefore my heart is glad and my tongue rejoices;
my body also will rest in hope,
²⁷ because you will not abandon me to the realm of the dead,
you will not let your holy one see decay.
²⁸ You have made known to me the paths of life;
you will fill me with joy in your presence.'

[29] "Fellow Israelites, I can tell you confidently that the patriarch David died and was buried, and his tomb is here to this day. [30] But he was a prophet and knew that God had promised him on oath that he would place one of his descendants on his throne. [31] Seeing what was to come, he spoke of the resurrection of the Messiah, that he was not abandoned to the realm of the dead, nor did his body see decay. [32] God has raised this Jesus to life, and we are all witnesses of it.

24 Contrary to what His enemies expected, God raised Jesus from the dead, freeing Him from the agony of death, because it was impossible for death to keep its hold on Him. Without doubt the resurrection proved the deity of Jesus. That was the main theme of Peter's sermon. "After spending one verse each on Christ's life and death, he spends nine verses on His resurrection."[2]

25 Peter was not making this up. To buttress what Peter had been saying, he quoted Psalm 16:8-11. This passage clarifies why God raised Jesus from the dead. It records what David prophetically wrote about Christ: "'I saw the Lord always before me. Because he is at my right hand, I will not be shaken." Jesus realized that God was at His right hand and would not be shaken by anything.

26 This verse expresses confidence in the face of death. Since Christ's confidence was in God, the cross could not dampen His joy. "Therefore my heart is glad and my tongue rejoices; my body also will rest in hope." His body would live in the hope of resurrection. He endured the cross because of the joy that was set before Him (Hebrews 12:2).

27 Another reason for Christ's confidence is that God would not abandon Him to the realm of the dead. He would not let His Holy One see decay. He would not remain a captive in the realm of the dead. Just before Jesus died, He committed His Spirit to His Father. When Jesus was in the tomb for three days, His body did not decay or see corruption.

28 "You have made known to me the paths of life; you will fill me with joy in your presence." TLB puts it this way: "You will give me back my life, and give me wonderful joy in your presence." This is a messianic statement. In fact, all Scripture bears witness to Christ. Its character is to support Christ's death, resurrection, and worldwide mission. Life means more than a mere escape from death but a joyful departure into the presence of God.

29 "Fellow Israelites, I can tell you confidently that the patriarch David died and was buried, and his tomb is here to this day." The honorific title "patriarch" for David confirms Peter's reference for the former king. David's tomb provides the evidence that he did not fulfill Psalm 16 just quoted. He experienced no resurrection. The quoted passage was messianic and was rightly applicable to Jesus as Peter did.

30 But David was a prophet and knew that God had promised him by an oath that He would place one of his descendants on his throne. The promise made to David is found in 2 Samuel 7:11-16. It was to have literal fulfillment. The Messiah would be one of David's descendants according to the flesh. From David would come the Messiah, who would sit on David's throne.

31 Seeing what was to come, David spoke of the resurrection of the Messiah, that He was not abandoned to the realm of the dead, nor did His body see decay. "Peter's argument from Psalm 16 can be summarized as follows: The psalm speaks of a resurrection. Since David, however, was not resurrected, it cannot speak of him. Thus, David speaks in the psalm of the Messiah. Hence, Messiah will rise from the dead."[3]

32 Peter concludes this portion of his sermon by saying, "God has raised this Jesus to life, and we are all witnesses of it." Peter had at least 120 disciples that witnessed Jesus' resurrection (Acts 1:15). Paul said at least 500 believers witnessed Jesus' resurrection (1 Corinthians 15:6). His resurrection is the guarantee of our own resurrection.

The Exaltation of Christ

Verses 33-36: Exalted to the right hand of God, he has received from the Father the promised Holy Spirit and has poured out what you now see and hear. [34] For David did not ascend to heaven, and yet he said,

"'The Lord said to my Lord:
"Sit at my right hand
35 until I make your enemies
a footstool for your feet."
36 "Therefore let all Israel be assured of this: God has made this Jesus, whom
you crucified, both Lord and Messiah."

33 Jesus was not only alive from the dead, He was exalted to the right hand of God, the place of power and glory. It is a position of universal rule and authority. From that position, Jesus had received from the Father the promised Holy Spirit and has poured out what they now saw and heard. He was responsible for what they were witnessing now.

34,35 For David did not ascend to heaven, and yet he said, "The Lord said to my Lord: 'Sit at my right hand until I make your enemies a footstool for your feet.'" Peter did not proclaim the exaltation of Jesus in a vacuum. He quoted another psalm of David (Psalm 110:1) to prove Christ's exaltation. David not only prophesied about the resurrection of Christ, but also about His exaltation. We are also seated spiritually with Christ at the right hand of God (Ephesians 2:6). That is the place of victory and triumph.

36 "Therefore let all Israel be assured of this: God has made this Jesus, whom you crucified, both Lord and Messiah." Peter was affirming that without a doubt, Jesus was their promised Messiah who they killed out of ignorance. Luke uses the title "Messiah" or "Christ" for Jesus for some twenty-five times in Acts. That same Jesus was enthroned as both Lord and Christ. What was prophesied had been fulfilled in Jesus. This was the only possible conclusion.

NOTES

1. John MacArthur, *The MacArthur New Testament Commentary: Acts 1-12* (Chicago, IL: Moody Publishers, 1994), p. 59.
2. Ibid., p. 64.
3. Ibid., p. 67.

Chapter 5

PETER'S SERMON – PART 2

Acts 2:37-47

Response to Peter's Sermon

Verses 37-41: When the people heard this, they were cut to the heart and said to Peter and the other apostles, "Brothers, what shall we do?" [38] Peter replied, "Repent and be baptized, every one of you, in the name of Jesus Christ for the forgiveness of your sins. And you will receive the gift of the Holy Spirit. [39] The promise is for you and your children and for all who are far off—for all whom the Lord our God will call." [40] With many other words he warned them; and he pleaded with them, "Save yourselves from this corrupt generation." [41] Those who accepted his message were baptized, and about three thousand were added to their number that day.

37 When the people heard Peter's great sermon, they were cut to the heart. They recognized their guilt. They were convinced and overcome by remorse. Conviction is the work of the Holy Spirit in our heart. The people said to Peter and the other apostles, "Brothers, what shall we do?" What could they do to be at peace with God, their Maker? This is a basic question every person searching for the truth must ask. This was the question Paul asked when he encountered the Lord on the road to Damascus (Acts 22:10). It was the same question the Philippian jailer asked Paul and Silas (Acts 16:30).

38 Peter replied, "Repent and be baptized, every one of you, in the name of Jesus Christ for the forgiveness of your sins. And you will receive the gift of the Holy Spirit." What they should do is threefold. First, they needed to repent individually. To repent simply means changing one's mind. Peter wanted them to change their minds about Jesus and to see their need for Him. Second, they needed baptism for the forgiveness of their sins. Baptism would mean identifying with Christ. Through baptism, our old life is buried and we rise out of the water as new persons in Christ. Third, they needed receiving the gift of the Holy Spirit because they would need Him to empower them for service.

39 The promise of the Holy Spirit was for them and their children and for all who are far off—for all whom the Lord our God will call. The promise of the Father was to send the Holy Spirit (Acts 1:4). It was not confined to those in Peter's audience. It embraced those who were far off, even to the Gentiles and to us today. Thus, the promise is extended and inclusive both in time ("your children") and in space ("all who are far off").

40 With many other words he warned them; and he pleaded with them, "Save yourselves from this corrupt generation." Beyond what is recorded here, Peter engaged in exhortation with the people. He urged them to separate themselves from national sin and from their present generation who were on their path of utter destruction. They must cease to identify themselves with the unbelieving Jews who crucified their Messiah.

41 Peter's sermon was great and impressive. It gave instant results. The Holy Spirit moved mightily in the hearts of those who heard him. Those who obeyed and accepted his message were baptized, and about three thousand were added to their number that day. Jesus had told His disciples that they would do greater works than He (John 14:12-18). Apparently, the Upper Room was too small for the new converts. They would have more space in the temple.

The First Church

*Verses 42-47: They devoted themselves to the apostles' teaching and to fellowship, to the breaking of bread and to prayer. *[43]* Everyone was filled with awe at the many wonders and signs performed by the apostles. *[44]* All the believers were together and had everything in common. *[45]* They sold property and possessions to give to anyone who had need. *[46]* Every day they continued* *to meet together in the temple courts. They broke bread in their homes and ate together with glad and sincere hearts, ⁴⁷ praising God and enjoying the favor of all the people. And the Lord added to their number daily those who were being saved.*

42 In order to grow, the disciples forming the church of Christ devoted themselves to following four things:

- *To the apostles' teaching*: This consists of God's Word and what Jesus taught the apostles. They were committed to the Word to guide their conduct and character. For believers to grow, they must be devoted to studying God's Word.
- *To fellowship*: Fellowship (*koinonia*, Greek) means "sharing." We must not isolate ourselves from other believers (Hebrews 10:25). A believer must participate in a local church to grow properly.
- *To the breaking of bread*: One of the key apostolic doctrines is the breaking of bread. It is the celebration of the Lord's Supper or Communion. Jesus commanded that we do this in His remembrance (1 Corinthians 11:24). We must regularly observe it.
- *To prayer*. Believers must constantly engage in the spiritual exercise of corporate prayer. Prayer is the divine rule for living. It is the means through which we let God get involved in our lives.

These are basic activities of the early church. Many churches today lack in some of these activities.

43 Everyone was filled with awe at the many wonders and signs performed by the apostles. "Awe" describes the attitude of reverence of the people had when they sensed God's presence. They were terrified by the supernatural nature of the church. The signs and wonders were designed to attract their attention and draw them to the Lord. God still performs miracles today when His people pray.

44 All the believers were together in one place (v. 46) and had everything in common. This was not the communist ideal, even though that ideal is noble. Communism breaks down because it leaves God out of the picture. What the disciples did here was totally voluntary and motivated by love for one another. It was simply caring and sharing with love. It emphasizes the unity and harmony of the early Christian community.

45 They sold property and possessions to give to anyone who had need. The practice of sharing possessions was common in the early church, including material things. When someone saw a need and was moved by the Spirit to help, the person sold a property to meet the need. The modern church needs to imitate this heart of generosity and concern for the real needs of others.

46 Every day they continued to meet together in the temple courts. Since the Upper Room was too small for them, they met in temple courts. They also met in homes. They broke bread in their homes and ate together with glad and sincere hearts. They were happy (Psalm 144:15). From what we are told, there appeared to be no complaining, no strife, no envy, no rivalry. The fruit of the Spirit was present (Galatians 5:22, 23).

47 They praised God and enjoyed the favor of all the people. To praise God means to exalt Him by reciting His works and attributes. Doing that produces joy among the people. The church had a good testimony among the unbelieving Jews because of the way they loved each other and served the Lord. And the Lord added to their number daily those who were being saved. Day by day people were being saved as they heard the gospel. The Lord Himself produced growth in the church. As Paul said, "I planted the seed, Apollos watered it, but God made it grow. So neither he who plants nor he who waters is anything, but only God who makes things grow"(1 Corinthians 3:6, 7).

Chapter 6

PETER HEALS A LAME BEGGAR

Acts 3:1-10

The Scene

Verses 1-3: One day Peter and John were going up to the temple at the time of prayer—at three in the afternoon. ² Now a man who was lame from birth was being carried to the temple gate called Beautiful, where he was put every day to beg from those going into the temple courts. ³ When he saw Peter and John about to enter, he asked them for money.

1 Luke presents an example of the "many wonders and miraculous signs" that were done by the apostles (Acts 2:43). One day Peter and John were going up to the temple at the time of prayer—at three in the afternoon. Peter and John were formerly fishermen and were partners in the ministry. "By nature and temperament they were different. Peter was a doer, John was a dreamer; Peter was a motivator, John was a mystic; Peter had his feet on the rock, John had his head in the clouds."[1] Together with James, John's brother, they formed the inner circle of Jesus' disciples.

It was 3 pm, the time for a prayer meeting at the temple, where believers gathered in Jesus' name. The Jews prayed at 9am, 12 noon, and 3 pm every day. Although these were now believers in Jesus Christ, they still observed the Jewish traditional prayer times as devout Jews. We must be men and women of prayer if we want God to use us.

2 Providentially, a man who was lame from birth was at the temple gate. He could not stand or walk. He had been a beggar for a long time.

He was now over forty years old (Acts 4:22). His case was pathetic and hopeless since no doctor could cure him. He was being carried to the temple gate called Beautiful, where he was put every day to beg for alms from those going into the temple courts. It was a perfect place to beg. One way for worshippers to show their devotion was to give alms to the beggar.

3 When he saw Peter and John about to enter the temple, he asked them for money. For the crippled man, begging was the only means of survival. He desperately needed help from others. All he was expecting from Peter and John was alms. He would soon realize that these two gentlemen were in touch with Jesus, the miracle-worker, the Lord of creation. The healing that follows shows what Jesus can do for the hopeless.

The Sign

Verses 4-8: Peter looked straight at him, as did John. Then Peter said, "Look at us!" *⁵ So the man gave them his attention, expecting to get something from them.* *⁶ Then Peter said, "Silver or gold I do not have, but what I do have I give you. In the name of Jesus Christ of Nazareth, walk."* *⁷ Taking him by the right hand, he helped him up, and instantly the man's feet and ankles became strong.* *⁸ He jumped to his feet and began to walk. Then he went with them into the temple courts, walking and jumping, and praising God.*

4 Peter and John looked intently at the beggar. They focused their attention on this poor crippled beggar. Then Peter said, "Look at us!" He was about to direct the beggar's attention from his religion to the Redeemer. He wanted there to be no doubt as to the source of the miracle. The man had been in this condition for so long so that God might be glorified.

5 So the man gave Peter and John his attention, expecting to get something from them. They would not give him a handout but something far more valuable. If we ask God for help, we must not be surprised when He gives us what we really need. God is sovereign over all things and works out all details according to His plan.

6 Then Peter said, "Silver or gold I do not have, but what I do have I give you. In the name of Jesus Christ of Nazareth, walk." Peter did not have money to give the beggar, but the beggar would receive far more than he could imagine. In the name of Jesus, the Messiah from Nazareth, Peter commanded the lame man to walk. Peter acted in Jesus' authority and with His delegated power.

A story is told of Thomas Aquinas who visited Pope Innocent II and found him counting a large sum of money. The Pope said to Thomas, "The church can no longer say, 'silver and gold have I none.'" Thomas replied, "That is true, Your Holiness, but then, neither can it now say, 'Arise and walk.'"[2]

7 Peter asked the man to exercise faith in Jesus. To encourage the man to start walking, Peter took him by the right hand and helped the man to get up. Instantly the man's feet and ankles became strong. The healing was not gradual but immediate. His symptoms were gone. Jesus is still in the healing business.

The attitude of most believers today toward healing is well expressed by John MacArthur when he wrote, "The gift of healing in the early church was limited to the apostles and their close associates in ministry. When they disappeared, so did the gift of healing."[3] This is not true and it does not have biblical support. God still heals today.

8 The man jumped to his feet and began to walk. Then he went with them into the temple courts, walking and jumping, and praising God. He was shouting, "Hallelujah! Praise the Lord!" His joy knew no bounds. He was free at last. All was changed. The man realized that the source of the healing was God, not Peter. He publicly identified himself with the apostles. He became a worshipper.

The Sequel

Verses 9,10: When all the people saw him walking and praising God, [10] they recognized him as the same man who used to sit begging at the temple gate called Beautiful, and they were filled with wonder and amazement at what had happened to him.

9,10 When all the people saw the formerly lame man walking and praising God, they recognized him as the same man who used to sit begging at the temple gate called Beautiful. People sensed that something marvelous and miraculous had just happened. They were filled with wonder and amazement at what had happened to him. It was undeniable that a miracle had taken place. Even the religious leaders, who were so much against Jesus, could not deny this miracle performed in His name (Acts 4:16).

NOTES

1. John Phillips, *Exploring Acts* (Grand Rapids, MI: Kregel Publications, 1986), p. 65.
2. Ibid., p. 68.
3. John MacArthur, *The MacArthur New Testament Commentary: Acts 1-12* (Chicago, IL: Moody Publishers, 1994), p. 97.

Chapter 7

PETER'S TESTIMONY BEFORE THE PEOPLE

Acts 3:11-26

Why Did it Happen?

Verses 11-16: While the man held on to Peter and John, all the people were astonished and came running to them in the place called Solomon's Colonnade. *[12] When Peter saw this, he said to them: "Fellow Israelites, why does this surprise you? Why do you stare at us as if by our own power or godliness we had made this man walk? [13] The God of Abraham, Isaac and Jacob, the God of our fathers, has glorified his servant Jesus. You handed him over to be killed, and you disowned him before Pilate, though he had decided to let him go. [14] You disowned the Holy and Righteous One and asked that a murderer be released to you. [15] You killed the author of life, but God raised him from the dead. We are witnesses of this. [16] By faith in the name of Jesus, this man whom you see and know was made strong. It is Jesus' name and the faith that comes through him that has completely healed him, as you can all see.*

11 "They all rushed out to Solomon's Hall, where he was holding tightly to Peter and John! Everyone stood there awed by the wonderful thing that had happened" (TLB). Solomon's Colonnade was at the eastern side of the temple. Jesus ministered there before (John 10:23). People were amazed at the miraculous healing of the lame beggar. The beggar was living proof of what Jesus could do through His disciples. The positive response of the people provided the launching pad for Peter's speech.

12 When Peter saw this, he seized the opportunity to preach Christ. He said to them: "Fellow Israelites, why does this surprise you? Why do you stare at us as if by our own power or godliness we had made this man walk?" Peter started by asking two questions. First, why should this incident surprise them? They should know as fellow Israelites that Jehovah is a miracle-working God. The fact that God was working a miracle through the apostles should cause no surprise. Second, why should they look at them as if their power had done this? Peter redirected their attention to Jesus, who was really responsible for the healing.

Chuck Smith wrote, "Two temptations occur whenever God begins to exercise the gifts of the Spirit: one, the crowd is tempted to exalt the instrument; and two, the instrument is tempted to receive the glory."[1] Paul said, "I have been crucified with Christ; it is no longer I who live, but Christ lives in me" (Galatians 2:20). Peter understood this truth too. Our chief end is to glorify God and serve Him forever.

13 Peter let the crowd know that the God of Abraham, Isaac and Jacob, the God of our fathers, has glorified His servant Jesus. You handed Him over to be killed, and you disowned Him before Pilate, though he had decided to let Him go. Peter referred to the God of their ancestors to stir reverence in their hearts. He contrasted what God did to His servant Jesus to what the people of Israel did to Him. The God of the covenant glorified Jesus by exalting Him to a position of honor, while the people handed Him over to be killed. The people were responsible for arresting, disowning, and executing Him.

Peter alluded to the suffering servant of Isaiah 52:13. The servant nature of Jesus' ministry implied that He willingly gave Himself unto death for His people.

14 Peter pressed home his point against His fellow Jews. He continued by saying, "You disowned the Holy and Righteous One and asked that a murderer be released to you." Peter boldly confronted his audience with their sin. They asked for the release of Barabbas, a murderer, instead of Jesus, the Righteous One. They rejected the Holy One (Psalm 16:10). "He came to that which was his own, but his own did not receive him" (John 1:11).

15 "You killed the author of life, but God raised him from the dead. We are witnesses of this." Jesus is the Author or Originator of Life. He claimed to be the source of life (John 5:6; 14:6). There was no one in Peter's audience who did not owe this life to Him. Though His own people crucified Him, God raised Him from the dead. The apostles were witnesses to the fact that Jesus was alive.

16 "By faith in the name of Jesus, this man whom you see and know was made strong. It is Jesus' name and the faith that comes through him that has completely healed him, as you can all see." The miracle was done by exercising faith in Jesus' name. The name of Jesus is not a magic word but it refers to the character and nature of Jesus. Peter did not take any credit for the healing. He and John were ordinary men.

A Call to Repentance

Verses 17-21: "Now, fellow Israelites, I know that you acted in ignorance, as did your leaders. ¹⁸ But this is how God fulfilled what he had foretold through all the prophets, saying that his Messiah would suffer. ¹⁹ Repent, then, and turn to God, so that your sins may be wiped out, that times of refreshing may come from the Lord, ²⁰ and that he may send the Messiah, who has been appointed for you—even Jesus. ²¹ Heaven must receive him until the time comes for God to restore everything, as he promised long ago through his holy prophets.

17 Peter expressed his knowledge of their acting in ignorance, as did their leaders. Jesus prayed for those who crucified Him because they acted out of ignorance (Luke 23:34). Ignorance arose from hardness of heart. Sins committed in ignorance are distinguished from willful or deliberate sins (Numbers 15:22-31). The ignorance of the people could be overlooked if they repent and turn to Christ for forgiveness.

18 "But this is how God fulfilled what he had foretold through all the prophets, saying that his Messiah would suffer." To every truth, there are human and divine views. The human view of Christ's suffering is that it was caused by the ignorance and unbelief of those who crucified Him. The divine view is that He suffered to fulfill what God had foreordained and made known through His prophets (e.g. Psalm 22, Isaiah 50:6; 53:1-12). Human execution of the Messiah could not thwart God's purposes. God worked through the evil intentions of people to fulfill His plan.

19 Peter did not leave his hearers without hope. He encouraged them to repent from their sins and turn to God. One of their sins in this case refers to their rejection and execution of Jesus. Repentance is the required response God expects from us when we sin. It leads to three blessings. First, God wipes out our sins. It is glorious to know that our sins can be wiped or blotted out. Second, times of refreshing come from the Lord. Without repentance, there is no refreshing.

20 Third, another blessing of repentance is that it would enable God send His appointed Messiah—even Jesus. If the entire nation repented and believed, the Messiah would return and establish His kingdom. But the nation did not repent. For individuals who repent and believe, Jesus would come into their lives and provide salvation. Jesus was here the first time to redeem humanity; His second coming will complete the process of redemption.

21 Heaven must receive Him until the time comes for God to restore all things at the end of the age, as He promised long ago through His holy prophets. Jesus will remain in heaven until all that God has spoken through the prophets is fulfilled. This may refer to the final era of salvation, the second coming of Christ. "The first coming of Christ marked the beginning of the period of restoration, and the second coming marks the end of the period."[2]

A Prophet Like Moses

Verses 22-26: For Moses said, 'The Lord your God will raise up for you a prophet like me from among your own people; you must listen to everything he tells you. [23] Anyone who does not listen to him will be completely cut off from their people.' [24] "Indeed, beginning with Samuel, all the prophets who have spoken have foretold these days. [25] And you are heirs of the prophets and of the covenant God made with your fathers. He said to Abraham, 'Through your offspring all peoples on earth will be blessed.' [26] When God raised up his servant, he sent him first to you to bless you by turning each of you from your wicked ways."

22 Peter began to cite biblical authority to support what he was saying. He first cited Moses as an example of God's holy prophet through whom He spoke. Moses said, "The Lord your God will raise up for you a prophet like me from among your own people; you must listen to everything he tells you." This quotation is from Deuteronomy 18:15. The religious leaders once asked John the Baptist if he was the prophet, but denied the claim (John 1:21-23). The promised prophet had come. Jesus was the prophet.

23 Just as the Israelites obeyed Moses, the lawgiver and leader, so people now must obey Christ as the Lawgiver, their Leader, the King, and their Prophet. The consequences of rejecting the Moses-like prophet are serious. Moses warned against disobeying Christ. "Anyone who does not listen to him will be completely cut off from their people." This is quoted from Deuteronomy 18:19. Peter added this quote to underline the seriousness of not listening to the prophet. Rejecting the prophet would mean forfeiting the covenant blessings.

24 Next, Peter cited Samuel and other prophets. Besides Moses, all the other prophets had foretold these days. What they prophesied about had now taken place. Samuel was the last judge in Israel, but he was also regarded as a prophet (1 Samuel 3:20). It was Samuel who anointed David as king and it was through David's greater Son that all the prophecies were fulfilled.

25 The people are heirs or children of the prophets and of the covenant God made with their fathers. They were living in the days that were spoken by the prophets. Peter cited the covenant God made with Abraham. He said to Abraham, "Through your offspring all peoples on earth will be blessed." This is in Genesis 12:1-3. That covenant saw its ultimate fulfillment in Jesus. All the nations of the earth will share in blessings promised to Abraham when they stand united to Christ.

26 When God raised up His servant, He sent Him first to them to bless them by turning each of them from their wicked ways. The phrase "raised up" does not refer to Jesus' resurrection but to His incarnation. God chose and sent Jesus to the Jews first. The message of salvation first came to the Jews (Romans 1:6). Being familiar with the prophecies concerning

Christ, they should have recognized Him when He came. It was necessary for Peter's hearers to repent and turn from their wicked ways.

NOTES

1. Chuck Smith, *The Book of Acts* (Costa Mesa, CA: The Word for Today, 2013), p. 54.
2. H. Leo Boles, *Acts* (Nashville, TN: Gospel Advocate Co., 1989), p. 60.

Chapter 8

PETER AND JOHN BEFORE THE AUTHORITIES

Acts 4:1-22

Peter and John Arrested

Verses 1-7: The priests and the captain of the temple guard and the Sadducees came up to Peter and John while they were speaking to the people. ² They were greatly disturbed because the apostles were teaching the people, proclaiming in Jesus the resurrection of the dead. ³ They seized Peter and John and, because it was evening, they put them in jail until the next day. ⁴ But many who heard the message believed; so the number of men who believed grew to about five thousand. ⁵ The next day the rulers, the elders and the teachers of the law met in Jerusalem. ⁶ Annas the high priest was there, and so were Caiaphas, John, Alexander and others of the high priest's family. ⁷ They had Peter and John brought before them and began to question them: "By what power or what name did you do this?"

1 In Chapter 4, Luke records the first persecution of the early church. As Peter and John were speaking to the people, the priests and the captain of the temple guard and the Sadducees came up to them. The priests were the Levites who conducted sacrifices in the temple. They were organized into twenty-four groups who ministered on a rotation basis. The captain of the temple guard was the leader of the temple police force. The Sadducees were a highly influential religious sect. The priests were concerned because of *where* Peter was preaching, while the Sadducees were involved because of *what* Peter was preaching.

2 Remembering what happened to Jesus a few months ago, they were greatly disturbed because the apostles were teaching the people, proclaiming in Jesus the resurrection of the dead. Peter and John had no credentials to teach the people since they were not formally trained. The religious leaders executed Jesus as a blasphemer, and now His disciples were teaching that He resurrected. (The Sadducees did not believe in resurrection.)

3 Because they were unable to tolerate the teaching of the apostles, they seized Peter and John. Because it was evening, they put them in jail until the next day. The whole incident started at 3pm and it was now evening. "The fact that it was evening meant it was too late to convene the Sanhedrin for a trial that day, and Jewish law did not permit trials at night (though that regulation was ignored in the case of Jesus)."[1] Peter and John did not resist but willingly submitted themselves to the authorities, knowing God was on their side.

4 They could bind the messengers, but they could not bind the message. In spite of the arrest, many who heard the message believed. The number of men who had believed since Pentecost was about five thousand (not counting women and children). The action of the religious leaders could not stop many from turning to Christ. Persecution always leads to the expansion of the church. "Communist Russia, China, and Cuba (to mention only a few) have all tried to suppress the preaching of Christ and all have failed."[2]

5,6 The next day the rulers, the elders and the teachers of the law met in Jerusalem. The rulers consisted of the ruling class of wealthy aristocrats such as the Sadducees. The elders were the respected representatives of the people of Israel. The teachers of the law were mainly Pharisees. Annas was the former high priest (A.D. 6-15) and he was deposed by the Romans. Joseph Caiaphas was the current high priest (A.D. 18-36) and was the son-in-law of Annas. John and Alexander were unknown.

The whole Sanhedrin gathered together to listen to Peter and John. The Sanhedrin consisted of seventy-two members, with the high priest Caiaphas serving as the president. It was the highest court of the Jewish nation. Just a few months ago, the Sanhedrin successfully executed Jesus. Now they wanted to get rid of His disciples.

7 They had Peter and John brought before them and began to question them: "By what power or what name did you do this?" The Sanhedrin wanted to know by what power Peter and John healed the lame beggar. Apparently, they did not grant Peter and John any authority to act or teach in the temple. Jesus was condemned by the religious leaders as a blasphemer. For the disciples to do anything in His name would make the leaders guilty of persecuting the disciples.

Peter's Testimony

Verses 8-12: Then Peter, filled with the Holy Spirit, said to them: "Rulers and elders of the people! ⁹ If we are being called to account today for an act of kindness shown to a man who was lame and are being asked how he was healed, ¹⁰ then know this, you and all the people of Israel: It is by the name of Jesus Christ of Nazareth, whom you crucified but whom God raised from the dead, that this man stands before you healed. ¹¹ Jesus is "'the stone you builders rejected, which has become the cornerstone.' ¹² Salvation is found in no one else, for there is no other name under heaven given to mankind by which we must be saved."

8 Peter and John spent the last night in prison. They must have been praying for God to take control of their defense the following morning. As a result, Peter was filled with the Holy Spirit and was able to display great courage. "There's nothing more exciting in all of life than to be filled with the Spirit, led by the Spirit, and used by the Spirit to accomplish His eternal purpose."[3]

Peter addressed the Sanhedrin with appropriate respect as "rulers and elders of the people." With confidence, he was able to stand before the most powerful spiritual leaders in the land.

9,10 "If we are being called to account today for an act of kindness shown to a man who was lame and are being asked how he was healed, then know this, you and all the people of Israel: It is by the name of Jesus Christ of Nazareth, whom you crucified but whom God raised from the dead, that this man stands before you healed." Peter made them to understand that they were arrested for doing good to a needy person. He courageously told the council that the ex-lame man was healed in Jesus' name. He now put them on trial and declared them guilty. He put the blame for the crucifixion of Christ on the council.

11 Jesus is "the stone you builders rejected, which has become the cornerstone." This is quoted from Psalm 118:22. Jesus Himself quoted it in His parable of the tenants (Mark 12:10). The religious leaders were supposed to be the builders of the nation, and yet they cast away the most important stone. Though they rejected Christ and executed Him, God had made Him the cornerstone through His resurrection. Though the spiritual leaders refuse to believe it, the resurrection of Jesus was a proven fact among the residents of Jerusalem.

12 "Salvation is found in no one else, for there is no other name under heaven given to mankind by which we must be saved." This is an often quoted verse. It declares that there is salvation in no other name except Jesus. This agrees with what Jesus said in John 14:6: "I am the way and the truth and the life. No one comes to the Father except through me." Jesus is not just an answer to human problems, He is the answer. He is the exclusive means of salvation. As John MacArthur said, "The exclusivism of Christianity goes against the grain of our religious pluralistic society... Christians preach an exclusive Christ in an inclusive age. Because of that, we are often accused of being narrow-minded, even intolerant."[4]

Response to Peter's Testimony

Verses 13-17: When they saw the courage of Peter and John and realized that they were unschooled, ordinary men, they were astonished and they took note that these men had been with Jesus. [14] But since they could see the man who had been healed standing there with them, there was nothing they could say. [15] So they ordered them to withdraw from the Sanhedrin and then conferred together. [16] "What are we going to do with these men?" they asked. "Everyone living in Jerusalem knows they have performed a notable sign, and we cannot deny it. [17] But to stop this thing from spreading any further among the people, we must warn them to speak no longer to anyone in this name."

13 When they saw the courage of Peter and John and realized that they were unschooled, ordinary men, they were astonished. It is not true that the apostles were uneducated. They were trained for three years by the great Teacher. They spoke as if they had been highly trained and they were. The council members were surprised at the unexpected boldness and confidence of the apostles before a daunting audience. They took note that these men had been with Jesus; they talked like Jesus and acted like Him. The secret of the Christian life is that Christ lives in us.

14 But since they could see the man who had been healed standing there with them, there was nothing they could say for the moment. The healed man could have disappeared with the crowd a day before, but he preferred to be with the Lord's people. Without saying anything, he added his own testimony, the testimony of a transformed life.

15 So they ordered the apostles and the healed man to withdraw from the Sanhedrin and then conferred together. This would prevent the three fellows from seeing the confusion of the leaders. It would be embarrassing to bring these men before the Sanhedrin and let them go without a charge. They found themselves in a dilemma, a difficult situation. They probably discussed this for a while during the council's recess.

16 "What are we going to do with these men?" they asked. This is a hard question. "Everyone living in Jerusalem knows they have performed a notable sign, and we cannot deny it." They could not deny the healing of the lame beggar. The miraculous healing was the talk of the town; everybody in Jerusalem knew about it. The council knew the truth, and yet they refused to admit it.

17 "But to stop this thing from spreading any further among the people, we must warn them to speak no longer to anyone in this name." The council felt they must take action to prevent the teaching of the apostles from spreading further. They must silence the apostles and stop the spread of Jesus' name. Their priority was not to get the truth but to prevent the truth from spreading. Satan always uses force when other methods fail to work.

Apostles Released

Verses 18-22: Then they called them in again and commanded them not to speak or teach at all in the name of Jesus. ¹⁹ But Peter and John replied, "Which is right in God's eyes: to listen to you, or to him? You be the judges! ²⁰ As for us, we cannot help speaking about what we have seen and heard." ²¹ After further threats they let them go. They could not decide how to punish them, because all the people were praising God for what had happened. ²² For the man who was miraculously healed was over forty years old.

18 Then they called them in and commanded them not to speak or teach at all in the name of Jesus. Under no circumstances should the apostles teach in the name of Jesus. Rulers often think they can suppress the truth by suppressing the press, controlling the media, or banning books.

The NT teaches that we uphold governmental authority as a general rule (Romans 13:1; Hebrews 13:17). However, when the government asks that we do something morally wrong, we should disobey. "When civil or religious authorities forbid what God requires or require what God forbids, some form of civil disobedience, with acceptance of penal consequences, becomes inescapable."[5] This is what Shadrach, Meshach, and Abednego did when asked to worship Nebuchadnezzar's image. They disobeyed the king and refused to worship his image (Daniel 3).

19,20 But Peter and John replied, "Which is right in God's eyes: to listen to you, or to him? You be the judges! As for us, we cannot help speaking about what we have seen and heard." The apostles immediately let the Sanhedrin know that they would not obey their order. We can imagine Peter and John leaving the Sanhedrin that day determined to keep preaching Christ. They had decided to obey God rather than men under any circumstances and were prepared to suffer the consequences. Of course, the Sanhedrin could not tell them to obey men instead of God. Again, the Sanhedrin was in a dilemma.

21 After further threats, they let them go. They could not find any legitimate reason to detain them. They could not decide how to punish them, because all the people were praising God (except the Sanhedrin) for what had happened. They feared how the people might react if they took further action against them. All they could do was to threaten them with imprisonment if they failed to stop their witness. Later in Acts 5:40, the apostles were flogged at the orders of the Sanhedrin.

22 "For the man who was miraculously healed was over forty years old." Luke now supplies the age of the healed beggar to show the significance of the miracle. The man had had a birth defect for forty years and was well known for begging for a long time. All human cures had failed. The apostles with the power of the Holy Spirit had triumphed over the infirmity

NOTES

1. John MacArthur, *The MacArthur New Testament Commentary: Acts 1-12* (Chicago, IL: Moody Publishers, 1994), p. 130.
2. Derek Carlsen, *Faith & Courage: Commentary on Acts* (Arlington Heights, IL: Christian Liberty Press, 2000), p. 83.
3. Chuck Smith, *The Book of Acts* (Costa Mesa, CA: The Word for Today, 2013), p. 63.
4. John MacArthur, p. 135.
5. Derek W. H. Thomas, *Acts: Reformed Expository Commentary* (Phillipsburg, NJ: P&R Publishing Co., 2011), p. 103.

Chapter 9

PRAYER AND POSSESSIONS

Acts 4:23-37

Power in Group Prayer

Verses 23-28: On their release, Peter and John went back to their own people and reported all that the chief priests and the elders had said to them. ²⁴ When they heard this, they raised their voices together in prayer to God. "Sovereign Lord," they said, "you made the heavens and the earth and the sea, and everything in them. ²⁵ You spoke by the Holy Spirit through the mouth of your servant, our father David:

"'Why do the nations rage
and the peoples plot in vain?
26 The kings of the earth rise up
and the rulers band together
against the Lord
and against his anointed one.
²⁷ Indeed Herod and Pontius Pilate met together with the Gentiles and the people of Israel in this city to conspire against your holy servant Jesus, whom you anointed. ²⁸ They did what your power and will had decided beforehand should happen.

23 On their release, Peter and John went back to their own people, their close circle of friends in Christ. When restraints were removed, they gravitated toward their own company. This might not be the company of all believers because no building would contain 5,000 people. It might refer to the group that included the apostles. They reported to this company all that the chief priests and the elders had said to them. They received encouragement and solidarity from others.

24 When the other disciples heard this, they raised their voices together in prayer to God. We can learn a lot from this prayer, born out of service for the Lord. "Sovereign Lord," they said, "you made the heavens and the earth and the sea, and everything in them." In their prayer, they praised God for being who He is—the Sovereign Lord and maker of the heavens and earth (Psalm 146:6). They took comfort in the Sovereign Lord who knows all things, controls all things, and orchestrates all things.

25,26 Their prayer was based solidly on God's Word. God spoke by the Holy Spirit through the mouth of His servant, their father David: "'Why do the nations rage and the peoples plot in vain? The kings of the earth rise up and the rulers band together against the Lord and against his anointed one." This is quoted from Psalm 2:2. It shows that if nations and kings gang up against God, all their attempts will fail. It is foolish and futile for men to scheme against God. The enemies of God could not stop the forward movement of God's kingdom.

27 The rulers in mind included Herod and Pontius Pilate. Herod Antipas was appointed by the Romans to rule over Galilee. Pontius Pilate was the appointed Roman governor over Judea. Herod and Pilate met together with the Gentiles and the people of Israel in Jerusalem to conspire against God's holy servant Jesus, whom He anointed. These enemies got rid of Christ by crucifying Him, but God raised Him from the dead and exalted Him. Their conspiracy against Christ actually fulfilled God's eternal plan. The wrath of men shall always praise God (Psalm 76:10).

28 Herod and Pilate did what God's power and will had decided beforehand should happen. They were working according to God's predestined purpose. As John MacArthur well said, "God is the supreme historian who wrote all history before it ever began."[1] Nothing happens by chance. God has foreknowledge of things before they happen. He laughs at the plans of wicked kings who attempt to stand in His way (Psalm 2:4).

Two Prayer Requests

Verses 29-31: Now, Lord, consider their threats and enable your servants to speak your word with great boldness. ³⁰ Stretch out your hand to heal and perform signs and wonders through the name of your holy servant Jesus." ³¹ After they prayed, the place where they were meeting was shaken. And they were all filled with the Holy Spirit and spoke the word of God boldly.

29 The believers' praise turned to petition as they asked the Lord to consider the threats of the Sanhedrin and enable His servants to speak His word with great boldness. They did not ask God to destroy their enemies, take vengeance on their behalf or bring a harsh judgment against them. They asked for boldness to do the very thing the Sanhedrin forbade Peter and John to do. Even after a spiritual victory, Satan may try to discourage us; we must pray for continued boldness.

30 In addition to boldness, they asked that the Lord to stretch out His hand to heal and perform signs and wonders through the name of His holy servant Jesus. Signs and wonders are always needed to confirm the gospel message. The name of Jesus has never lost its power to perform miracles. Since God is the same yesterday, today, and forever (Hebrew 13:8), God still works miracles among believers who trust in Him to do so.

31 After they prayed, three things happened. First, the place where they were meeting was shaken. The room where they gathered shook as if an earthquake had taken place. The shaking was a visible manifestation of God. God granted their requests instantaneously. Second, they were all filled with the Holy Spirit. This shows that filling with the Holy Spirit is not a one time event. We must seek to be filled from time to time. Third, they spoke the word of God boldly. Their boldness came after the fullness of the Spirit. Instead of being silent or compromising the message, they became even bolder.

Believers Shared their Possessions

Verses 32-35: All the believers were one in heart and mind. No one claimed that any of their possessions was their own, but they shared everything they had. ³³ With great power the apostles continued to testify to the resurrection of the Lord Jesus. And God's grace was so powerfully at work in them all, ³⁴ that there were no needy persons among them. For from time to time those who owned land or houses sold them, brought the money from the sales ³⁵ and put it at the apostles' feet, and it was distributed to anyone who had need.

32 All the believers were one in heart and mind. No one claimed that any of their possessions were their own, but they shared everything they had in common. They focused on sharing what they had with others. This required love. Jesus told His disciples, "Your strong love for each other will prove to the world that you are my disciples" (John 13:35, TLB). Their love spilled over into sharing things.

33 With great power the apostles continued to testify to the resurrection of the Lord Jesus. The great power included God's anointing the apostles' message, confirming it with signs and wonders, and convicting the hearts of the hearers. They had the boldness to preach, contrary to what the Sanhedrin told them not to do. And God's grace was so powerfully at work in them all. God's grace is His enablement to perform the tasks He assigns.

34,35 The proof that God's grace was upon them was that there were no needy persons among them. For from time to time those who owned land or houses sold them, brought the money from the sales and put it at the apostles' feet, and it was distributed to anyone who had need. The better-off members generously shared with those who had much less. The motivation was Christian love, while the manifestation was voluntary sharing. Those who sold their land and houses did so voluntarily. The proceeds were distributed according to needs.

This fulfills Deuteronomy 15:4: "There should be no poor among, for in the land the LORD your God is giving you to possess as your inheritance, he will surely bless you." God blesses His people so that there is no poverty. Poverty is not God's perfect will for His people. Today, some Christians are poor because we don't follow God's way of doing things.

Barnabas, the Loyal Encourager

Verses 36,37: Joseph, a Levite from Cyprus, whom the apostles called Barnabas (which means "son of encouragement"), ³⁷ sold a field he owned and brought the money and put it at the apostles' feet.

36,37 Luke singles out Barnabas as an example of one of those who sold their properties. Joseph was better known as Barnabas (which means "son of encouragement"). His original name was Joseph, but he was called (or nicknamed) Barnabas by the apostles. He was a Levite, i.e. he was a descendant of the priestly tribe that performed temple duties. He was from Cyprus, which was an island off the south coast of Asia Minor. He sold a field he owned and brought the money and put it at the apostles' feet. We are not told whether Barnabas owned the land in Cyprus or Palestine. The Mosaic law forbade Levites to own land in Israel (Numbers 18:20; Deuteronomy 10:9).

Barnabas is mentioned at this point probably because of his roles later in Acts. He was the one who encouraged Paul during his early service for the Lord. Selfless sacrifice is the first account of him we have. He is a good example for us to emulate.

NOTES

1. John MacArthur, *The MacArthur New Testament Commentary: Acts 1-12* (Chicago, IL: Moody Publishers, 1994), p. 141.

Chapter 10

ANANIAS AND SAPPHIRA

Acts 5:1-11

The Deception by a Couple

Verses 1-2: Now a man named Ananias, together with his wife Sapphira, also sold a piece of property. ² With his wife's full knowledge he kept back part of the money for himself, but brought the rest and put it at the apostles' feet.

1 Barnabas was a good example of what it means to be a dedicated Christian. God uses people like Barnabas to bless His church. Just like Barnabas, a man named Ananias, together with his wife Sapphira, also sold a piece of property. The couple had witnessed Barnabas' generous giving and the respect it got from other believers. They wanted to follow suit. They wanted the praise of others without the corresponding sacrifice.

2 Unlike Barnabas, Ananias (meaning "God is merciful") kept back part of the money for himself with his wife's full knowledge. He brought the rest and put it at the apostles' feet. He pretended that he gave all the money he had received from the sale of their land. This was deception, dishonesty, and hypocrisy. We deceive others when we pretend we are more holy, more committed, more spiritual, and more generous than we really are.

The Deception Exposed

Verses 3-6: Then Peter said, "Ananias, how is it that Satan has so filled your heart that you have lied to the Holy Spirit and have kept for yourself some of the money you received for the land? ⁴ Didn't it belong to you before it was sold? And after it was sold, wasn't the money at your disposal? What made you think of doing such a thing? You have not lied just to human beings but to God." ⁵ When Ananias heard this, he fell down and died. And great fear seized all who heard what had happened. ⁶ Then some young men came forward, wrapped up his body, and carried him out and buried him.

3 Then Peter asked, "Ananias, how is it that Satan has so filled your heart that you have lied to the Holy Spirit and have kept for yourself some of the money you received for the land?" The deception of the couple did not fool the body of Christ. The Holy Spirit exposed the deception to Peter. Ananias and his wife had allowed Satan to make them lie to the Holy Spirit and keep back part of the money. When Satan cannot defeat the church from the outside by force, he attacks from the inside using falsehood. Lying and deception are some of his common weapons.

4 "Didn't it belong to you before it was sold? And after it was sold, wasn't the money at your disposal? What made you think of doing such a thing? You have not lied just to human beings but to God." Verse 3 says that Ananias lied to the Holy Spirit, while verse 4 says he lied to God. This indicates that God and the Holy Spirit are one. We should never presume that God or the Holy Spirit does not know all the details about us. When we lie to the church, we lie to God. Someone has said, "The story of Ananias is to the Book of Acts, what the story of Achan is to the Book of Joshua."

5 When Ananias heard this, he fell down and died. Death could be a divine judgment for a believer (1 Corinthians 11:30-32). Apparently, God intervened so quickly and punished deception. He made Ananias and his wife an example to remind the congregation of His holiness. As a result of the death of Ananias, "great fear seized all who heard what had happened."

6 Ananias' death was followed by burial. Some young men of the congregation came forward, wrapped up his body in a burial cloth, carried him out, and buried him outside the city. It was customary in some cultures to bury the corpse the same day the person died. "The corpse could not be left overnight within the city of Jerusalem but had to be buried before sundown according to Jewish law, based on Deut. 21:23."[1]

The Deception Further Exposed

Verses 7-11: About three hours later his wife came in, not knowing what had happened. [8] Peter asked her, "Tell me, is this the price you and Ananias got for the land?" "Yes," she said, "that is the price." [9] Peter said to her, "How could you conspire to test the Spirit of the Lord? Listen! The feet of the men who buried your husband are at the door, and they will carry you out also." [10] At that moment she fell down at his feet and died. Then the young men came in and, finding her dead, carried her out and buried her beside her husband. [11] Great fear seized the whole church and all who heard about these events.

7 About three hours later his wife Sapphira came in, not knowing what had previously happened. Sapphira means "beautiful." The atmosphere was pregnant with her coming in, but she suspected nothing. Her husband was dead and buried, and Sapphira knew nothing about it. She was looking for some praise and commendation.

8 Peter asked her, "Tell me, is this the price you and Ananias got for the land?" "Yes," she said, "that is the price." That was a lie and this was her sin. Peter gave her the opportunity to tell the truth, confess her sin and correct it, but she chose to persist in lying. She exposed herself as guilty of lying like her husband. She was an accomplice in the deception with her husband.

9 Peter said to her, "How could you conspire to test the Spirit of the Lord? Listen! The feet of the men who buried your husband are at the door, and they will carry you out also." She had tested the Lord's Spirit. She thought she and her husband could get away with it, presuming that nobody would know the difference.

10 At that moment she fell down at Peter's feet and died. God's judgment is always fair and just. He has the right to discipline His own. Sin must be dealt with decisively. The young men came in and, finding her dead, carried her out and buried her beside her husband. As Ananias and

Sapphira joined together to test the Lord, they were joined together in death. The normal customs of burial and mourning were not applied in this case of the guilty couple.

11 The news of the events spread quickly throughout the church and the wider community in the city of Jerusalem. As a result, great fear seized the whole church and all who heard about these events. (This is the first time the word "church" is used in Acts.) Church discipline always deters others from committing the same sin. The church had purged itself of deception. It is proper that judgment begins in the household of God (1 Peter 4:17).

NOTES

1. Steven Ger, *The Book of Acts: Witnesses to the World* (Chattanooga, TN: AMG Publishers, 2004), p. 85.

Chapter 11

THE APOSTLES PERSECUTED - PART 1

Acts 5:12-26

The Apostles Heal Many

Verses 12-16: The apostles performed many signs and wonders among the people. And all the believers used to meet together in Solomon's Colonnade.[13] No one else dared join them, even though they were highly regarded by the people. [14] Nevertheless, more and more men and women believed in the Lord and were added to their number. [15] As a result, people brought the sick into the streets and laid them on beds and mats so that at least Peter's shadow might fall on some of them as he passed by. [16] Crowds gathered also from the towns around Jerusalem, bringing their sick and those tormented by impure spirits, and all of them were healed.

12 The apostles performed many signs and wonders among the people. The signs and wonders were designed to confirm the gospel message and affirm that the apostles were true servants of God. One cannot read the book of Acts without yearning to see the same supernatural power as we see in the early church. Although it is rare, Christians still minister in the miraculous today. We must realize that God strongly desires to shower His blessings on the church so that we may keep winning the lost for Christ.

All the believers used to meet together on regular basis in Solomon's Colonnade, which was part of the temple complex build by King Herod. It was located on the eastern side of the temple.

13 Great fear was on all the unbelievers due to the power of God resting on the disciples. No one else dared join them, even though they were highly regarded by the people. The disciples of Christ were highly respected for their devotion and the power of God demonstrated through them. The believers were united together, but many of the unbelievers feared to be part of this body and kept their distance.

14 Nevertheless, more and more men and women believed in the Lord and were added to their number. The Lord Jesus demands total commitment from His disciples. "Only those who are willing to forsake all, including sin, and lose their lives in submission to Him, are worthy to be His followers. A church made up of such people will be a pure church, with a powerful testimony to the world."[1]

15 As a result of their total commitment to the Lord, people brought the sick into the streets and laid them on beds and mats so that at least Peter's shadow might fall on some of them as he passed by. God gave the apostles supernatural power to perform miracles. People believed that even Peter's shadow carried healing power. They recognized him as a man of God and believed that they could be healed through proximity to him. The Holy Spirit used a variety of ways to encourage people's faith.

16 Crowds gathered also from the towns around Jerusalem, bringing their sick and those tormented by impure spirits, and all of them were healed. It is important to note that all the sick people were healed. Although the apostles were primarily responsible for these healings, the ordinary members exercised the miraculous powers as well (Acts 6:8). The apostles ministered as their Lord has ministered and fulfilled the Lord's promise that they would do greater work (John 14:12-14).

The Apostles are Arrested

Verses 17-26: Then the high priest and all his associates, who were members of the party of the Sadducees, were filled with jealousy. [18] They arrested the apostles and put them in the public jail. [19] But during the night an angel of the Lord opened the doors of the jail and brought them out. [20] "Go, stand in the temple courts," he said, "and tell the people all about this new life." [21] At daybreak they entered the temple courts, as they had been told, and began to teach the people. When the high priest and his associates arrived, they called together the Sanhedrin—the full assembly of the elders of Israel—and sent to the jail for the apostles. [22] But on arriving at the jail, the officers did not find them there. So they went back and reported, [23] "We found the jail securely locked, with the guards standing at the doors; but when we opened them, we found no one inside." [24] On hearing this report, the captain of the temple guard and the chief priests were at a loss, wondering what this might lead to. [25] Then someone came and said, "Look! The men you put in jail are standing in the temple courts teaching the people." [26] At that, the captain went with his officers and brought the apostles. They did not use force, because they feared that the people would stone them.

17 Then the high priest and all his associates, who were members of the party of the Sadducees, were filled with jealousy. The high priest was likely Joseph Caiaphas. He was a Sadducee. He and his associates were jealous of the spectacular success of these "untrained" men and could no longer tolerate them. They probably figured out that if everyone followed the new way of the apostles, their positions of authority and wealth would be threatened. The living church was enjoying the new, while the dead council was protecting the old. It was the age-old conflict between the living God and Satan. As Satan used the religious leaders to oppose Jesus, he was now using them to oppose His disciples.

18 They organized a deliberate opposition to the way of truth. They arrested all the apostles and threw them into the public jail. The twelve apostles were involved in this case. They did not resist arrest but went along with the guards. The Sadducees treated them like common criminals and locked them up overnight so that they could be brought for trial the next day. They thought they could silence them by putting them in jail.

19 As mentioned earlier, what we have here is a clash of leaders—the leaders of the new order and the leaders of the old order. God intervened and confirmed His support for the leaders of the new order by sending an angel to deliver them. During the night an angel of the Lord opened the doors of the jail and brought the apostles out. This would embarrass the Sadducees who denied the existence of angels (Acts 23:8).

20 After releasing the apostles, the angel told them, "Go, stand in the temple courts and tell the people all about this new life." They were told to fearlessly continue their preaching in the temple. They were to go back to their usual place, boldly preaching the life-imparting gospel. The temple was the public and appropriate place to broadcast the gospel message. If God was for them, who could be against them?

21 At daybreak they entered the temple courts, as they had been told, and began to teach the people. Since they had God's backing, they were not afraid of the Sanhedrin. They preached early that morning for those who came for the morning sacrifice.

When the high priest and his associates arrived, they called together the Sanhedrin—the full assembly of the elders of Israel—and sent to the jail for the apostles. The "full assembly" might mean that all the seventy members were present. They were not aware of what had happened overnight. They wanted the apostles to be brought before them. If they could deal with Jesus, they would take care of His disciples also.

22 The officers (some of the temple police) were sent on a fruitless errand. On arriving at the jail, the officers did not find the apostles there. They could not figure out what happened. They must have been greatly surprised to see that the prisoners were gone. So they went back empty-handed and reported to the Sanhedrin.

23 The officers reported to the Sanhedrin and said, "We found the jail securely locked, with the guards standing at the doors; but when we opened them, we found no one inside." The guards must have been unconscious when the prisoners escaped. Twelve men had escaped, and nobody knew exactly where they were now. There was no sign of their escape.

24 On hearing this report, the captain of the temple guard and the chief priests were at a loss, wondering what this might lead to. They were embarrassed and confused. They felt powerless and incapable to control the apostles. The apostles had defied their authority by going back to the temple to preach. It was no part of Christianity to defy constituted authority except when the authority demanded what was wrong or contrary to God's will.

25 While they were still deliberating, someone came and said, "Look! The men you put in jail are standing in the temple courts teaching the people." Not only were the apostles no longer in custody, they were in the temple speaking in the name of Jesus. They were doing just what they had been forbidden to do.

26 The captain went with his officers and brought the apostles. They were "brought," not arrested. They did not use force, because they feared that the people would stone them. They did not even ask the apostles how they escaped. As before, the apostles offered no resistance; they willingly surrendered themselves to the arrest.

NOTES

1. John MacArthur, *The MacArthur New Testament Commentary: Acts 1-12* (Chicago, IL: Moody Publishers, 1994), p. 163.

Chapter 12

THE APOSTLES PERSECUTED - PART 2

Acts 5:27-42

Peter's Witness

Verses 27-32: The apostles were brought in and made to appear before the Sanhedrin to be questioned by the high priest. *28 "We gave you strict orders not to teach in this name," he said. "Yet you have filled Jerusalem with your teaching and are determined to make us guilty of this man's blood." 29 Peter and the other apostles replied: "We must obey God rather than human beings! 30 The God of our ancestors raised Jesus from the dead—whom you killed by hanging him on a cross. 31 God exalted him to his own right hand as Prince and Savior that he might bring Israel to repentance and forgive their sins. 32 We are witnesses of these things, and so is the Holy Spirit, whom God has given to those who obey him."*

27 The apostles were peaceably brought in and made to appear before the Sanhedrin's semicircle of judgment. They stood before the council to be questioned by the high priest, the president of the council. They knew that they had defied the authority of the council. They were not afraid to stand before the council because they realized that they were in the right.

28 "We gave you strict orders not to teach in this name," the high priest said. "Yet you have filled Jerusalem with your teaching and are determined to make us guilty of this man's blood." It seemed that the high priest could not mention the name of Jesus but could only refer to Him as "this man." The apostles were accused of disregarding the prior orders of the Sanhedrin. The high priest was speaking from a guilty conscience. He forgot when he along with the crowd said to Pilate: "Let his blood be on us and on our children" (Matthew 27:25). He was almost admitting that there was nothing they could do to stop all of Jerusalem from coming under the influence of this new teaching.

29 Peter and the other apostles replied: "We must obey God rather than human beings!" Presumably, Peter was the spokesman for the Twelve. The Sanhedrin's order not to preach the gospel was in direct conflict with God's will. So their order could not be obeyed by the apostles. To obey them would mean disobeying God. The apostles would not give in. They did not change their convictions and their message. Rather they obeyed God and trusted Him to take care of whatever might be the consequences. It was a question of loyalty.

30 The God of our ancestors raised Jesus from the dead—whom you killed by hanging Him on a cross. The apostles identified with their common heritage by using the term "the God of our ancestors." It was Abraham's God, Israel's God, and Moses' God who raised Jesus from the dead. The covenant-keeping God proved the religious leaders wrong by raising His Son from the grave. The apostles fearlessly told the council that they were guilty of killing the Messiah.

31 While the religious leaders thought they had disgraced, despised, and crucified Jesus, God exalted Him to His own right hand as Prince and Savior. The right hand of God is the position of honor and power. Jesus was the Prince or Pioneer and the Savior who saves from sin and judgment those who trust in Him. In fact, the name Jesus means "God is salvation." He came that He might bring Israel to repentance and forgive their sins. Repentance involves turning away from sin. Forgiveness has to do with pardoning for an offense or sin.

32 The apostles were eyewitnesses of these things. So is the Holy Spirit, the chief witness, whom God has given to those who obey him (1 John 5:7). They were now dealing with the Holy Spirit. It was the Holy Spirit who enabled the apostles to give a bold witness before the council. They were commissioned to declare what they have witnessed before all people.

They did that fearlessly, walking in the footsteps of Daniel and his associates (Daniel 3,6).

Gamaliel's Advice

Verses 33-40: When they heard this, they were furious and wanted to put them to death. ³⁴ But a Pharisee named Gamaliel, a teacher of the law, who was honored by all the people, stood up in the Sanhedrin and ordered that the men be put outside for a little while. ³⁵ Then he addressed the Sanhedrin: "Men of Israel, consider carefully what you intend to do to these men. ³⁶ Some time ago Theudas appeared, claiming to be somebody, and about four hundred men rallied to him. He was killed, all his followers were dispersed, and it all came to nothing. ³⁷ After him, Judas the Galilean appeared in the days of the census and led a band of people in revolt. He too was killed, and all his followers were scattered. ³⁸ Therefore, in the present case I advise you: Leave these men alone! Let them go! For if their purpose or activity is of human origin, it will fail. ³⁹ But if it is from God, you will not be able to stop these men; you will only find yourselves fighting against God." ⁴⁰ His speech persuaded them. They called the apostles in and had them flogged. Then they ordered them not to speak in the name of Jesus, and let them go.

33 The Sanhedrin was not interested in learning the truth. All they wanted was to keep things they way they were and protect their interests. When they heard the apostles, they were furious. They would have killed the apostles if not for the intervention of Gamaliel. The message was convicting enough to make the council angry. The word of God is sharper than a two-edged sword (Hebrews 4:12). There are three ways people react to the conviction of the Holy Spirit—hostility, indifference, or acceptance.

34 Gamaliel, a Pharisee, a teacher of the law, who was honored by all the people, stood up in the Sanhedrin and ordered that the apostles be removed from the chamber for a little while. His name means "God is also for me." He was of the Pharisee party. He was the grandson of Hillel the famous Hebrew scholar. Paul had boasted that he sat at Gamaliel's feet. He was apparently moderate in his approach. Gamaliel warned the council against taking extreme measures with the Christians.

35 After sending out the apostles for a while, Gamaliel addressed the Sanhedrin: "Men of Israel, consider carefully what you intend to do to these men." Gamaliel appealed to them to be cautious and take a wise, careful approach. Since they were acting as judges of Israel, they could come under God's judgment if they misjudged. If the Christian movement was from God, it would dangerous and foolish to take action against it.

36 Gamaliel reminded the council that revolutions come and go. He cited two examples to support this. In recent times, Theudas appeared, claiming to be somebody, and about four hundred men rallied to him. Nothing is known about this insurrectionist, Theudas. We know that many "liberators" surfaced in Palestine and Theudas could be one of them. The fact that he led a revolt in early first century is quite possible. He was killed, all his followers were dispersed, and it all came to nothing.

37 After him, Judas the Galilean appeared in the days of the census and led a band of people in revolt. Judas led a revolt against Rome when Quirinius ordered a census in A.D. 6. This census involved more than just counting people; it included paying tax to Rome. (This is the not the same census Luke records in Luke 2:2.) He too was killed, and all his followers were scattered.

38 Therefore, in the present case involving the apostles, Gamaliel advised the council to leave them alone! Let them go! For if their purpose or activity is of human origin, it will fail. In other words, if this Jesus movement is a human movement, it would surely disappear like those of Theudas and Judas. Gamaliel saw Jesus as another "liberator," attempting to set the nation of Israel free from Rome.

39 But if it is from God, it would be impossible for the council to stop these men. They would only find themselves fighting against God and blocking what He might be doing. If the movement is inspired by God, no one can fight against it and it will overcome human opposition. How do we react to new religious movements? It is better to be tolerant and accommodating rather than be hostile and repressive. As Lloyd Ogilvie said, "If they are of God we can't stop them. If not, they will not succeed anyhow!"[1]

40 Gamaliel's logical speech persuaded the council. They were convinced by what he said. Because of his rational approach, a compromise was reached. They called the apostles in and had them flogged. The law of Moses stipulated flogging when considered necessary (Deuteronomy 25:1-3). Then they ordered them not to speak in the name of Jesus, and let them go.

The Apostles Rejoice

Verses 41,42: The apostles left the Sanhedrin, rejoicing because they had been counted worthy of suffering disgrace for the Name. ⁴² Day after day, in the temple courts and from house to house, they never stopped teaching and proclaiming the good news that Jesus is the Messiah.

41 The flogging was meant to discourage and intimidate the apostles. It actually had the opposite effect. They saw it as sharing in the suffering of Christ. The apostles left the Sanhedrin, rejoicing because they had been counted worthy of suffering disgrace for the Name. What a difference it makes to know Jesus Christ. Jesus had taught them to expect persecution and to rejoice in it (Matthew 5:10-12; John 15:20). Like James says, "Count it all joy, my brethren, when you meet various trials" (James 1:2, RSV).

42 Day after day, in the temple courts and from house to house, the apostles never stopped teaching and proclaiming the good news that Jesus is the Messiah. They witnessed in the temple because that was where religious people gathered. The center of their witness was Jesus Christ. By consistently preaching the gospel, they were able to turn their world upside down (Acts 17:6). The Sanhedrin had lost twice in their opposition against the church of Christ.

NOTES

1. Lloyd J. Ogilvie, *Acts: The Communicator's Commentary* (Waco, TX: Word Books, 1983), p. 130.

Chapter 13

ANGELIC STEPHEN

Acts 6:1-15

The Appointment of the Seven

Verses 1-7: In those days when the number of disciples was increasing, the Hellenistic Jews among them complained against the Hebraic Jews because their widows were being overlooked in the daily distribution of food. ² So the Twelve gathered all the disciples together and said, "It would not be right for us to neglect the ministry of the word of God in order to wait on tables. ³ Brothers and sisters, choose seven men from among you who are known to be full of the Spirit and wisdom. We will turn this responsibility over to them ⁴ and will give our attention to prayer and the ministry of the word." ⁵ This proposal pleased the whole group. They chose Stephen, a man full of faith and of the Holy Spirit; also Philip, Procorus, Nicanor, Timon, Parmenas, and Nicolas from Antioch, a convert to Judaism. ⁶ They presented these men to the apostles, who prayed and laid their hands on them. ⁷ So the word of God spread. The number of disciples in Jerusalem increased rapidly, and a large number of priests became obedient to the faith.

1 As the first church grew rapidly in number, it needed proper organization and management. In those days when the number of disciples was increasing, the Hellenistic Jews among them complained against the Hebraic Jews because their widows were being overlooked in the daily distribution of food. This is fifth church-growth report in Acts (Acts 2:41; 2:47; 4:4; 5:14; 6:1).

There were two kinds of Jews in the early church. The Hellenistic (Greek-speaking) Jews were those of Diaspora; they had lived outside of Israel for years. The Hebraic Jews were native Palestinians and they spoke Hebrew or Aramaic. The Hellenistic Jews were in Jerusalem for the Passover and might have remained there to learn from the apostles. The dispute was between two kinds of Jews. The Greek-speaking Jews complained their widows were discriminated against in the daily distribution of food and supplies to the poor.

2 So the Twelve gathered all the disciples together and said, "It would not be right for us to neglect the ministry of the word of God in order to wait on tables." It would not make sense for the apostles or leaders in general to be doing what church members could do. It was not that the apostles were not humble enough to run errands for the church; it was a matter of prioritizing their time.

3 "Brothers and sisters, choose seven men from among you who are known to be full of the Spirit and wisdom. We will turn this responsibility over to them." The apostles asked the brethren to select seven men to take care of the food distribution. These men must meet four requirements. First, they must be men. The service was restricted to men by the culture of the day when women could not lead. But today women can be used of God if they make themselves available. Second, they must be "from among you." They must be born again and be part of the church. Third, they must be full of the Spirit. The Spirit would empower them to perform their duty well. Fourth, they must be full of wisdom. They needed practical wisdom to apply the Word of God to daily situations. They needed to be able to distinguish between genuine needs and wants.

4 The apostles understood their priority. They realized the amount of time and effort that was required to minister the Word properly. They could now give their primary attention to prayer and the ministry of the Word. The apostles would not let anything distract them from the primary duty of teaching the Word and prayer. Some pastors today are so occupied with the administrative details of running a church that they had little or no time for intercession and Bible study. Church leaders are called to equip God's people for the work of the ministry (Ephesians 4:12).

5 This proposal pleased the whole congregation. They chose Stephen, a man full of faith and of the Holy Spirit; also Philip, Procorus, Nicanor, Timon, Parmenas, and Nicolas from Antioch, a convert to Judaism. Stephen had a crucial role to play in spreading the gospel beyond Jerusalem. Philip was later responsible for taking the gospel to the Samaritans. His four daughters became prophetesses (Acts 21:8). He should not be confused with the apostle Philip of Bethsaida, who brought Nathanael to Jesus (John 1:43-45). We know nothing about the other five men.

Some have called these men the first church deacons, but they were never called deacons back then. However, the work of the Twelve and the work of the Seven are both called "ministry." The former is "the ministry of the word," while the latter "the ministry of tables." Both are different ways of serving God and His people.

6 The church nominated and presented these seven men to the apostles, who appointed them, and prayed for them, and laid their hands on them. This is the first time the phrase "laid their hands" is used in the NT. It signified identification of the apostles with these men and their ministry. It imparts the authority and privileges that accompany such an office. "Elders, deacons, and all who served in the early church were ordained this way."[1]

7 Once the apostles were freed up to carry out their primary duty, they could dedicate their energy to the ministry of the Word. As a result, the Word of God kept spreading. The number of disciples in Jerusalem increased rapidly. They lost count of the actual number. A large number of priests who ministered at the temple in Jerusalem became obedient to the faith. "This was a major breakthrough, since most of the priests were Sadducees, who did not believe in the resurrection of the dead."[2]

The Wisdom of Stephen

Verses 8-11: Now Stephen, a man full of God's grace and power, performed great wonders and signs among the people. [9] Opposition arose, however, from *members of the Synagogue of the Freedmen (as it was called)—Jews of Cyrene and Alexandria as well as the provinces of Cilicia and Asia—who began to argue with Stephen. ¹⁰ But they could not stand up against the wisdom the Spirit gave him as he spoke. ¹¹ Then they secretly persuaded some men to say, "We have heard Stephen speak blasphemous words against Moses and against God."*

8 Up till now, Luke has focused his writings on the activities of the apostles, especially Peter. Now Luke focuses on Stephen, one the Seven. Stephen was a man full of God's grace and power. He performed great wonders and signs among the people. This shows that performing signs and wonders is not limited to the apostles. Stephen was fully controlled by the Holy Spirit. "Stephen's ministry was the catalyst that catapulted the church out of Jerusalem into the rest of the world."[3]

9 Opposition arose, however, from members of the Synagogue of the Freedmen (as it was called)—Jews of Cyrene and Alexandria as well as the provinces of Cilicia and Asia—who began to argue with Stephen. The "Freedmen" were descendants of the Jews who were taken as slaves to Rome and had been pardoned to return to Israel as free men. They possibly formed their own synagogue in Jerusalem. Cyrene and Alexandria were cities in North Africa. Cyrene was the home of Simon who helped Jesus carry His cross (Luke 23:26). Jews from these three synagogues came and argued with Stephen.

10 But they could not stand up against the wisdom the Spirit gave Stephen as he spoke. He was a skilled debater. Their human reasoning could not cope with Stephen's Spirit-inspired wisdom. Here we see the disparity between the wisdom of man and the wisdom of God. Jesus had promised to provide His followers with help from the Holy Spirit and wisdom (Luke 12:12; 21:15). The Holy Spirit used Stephen to wield the Word of God, which is the sword of the Spirit.

11 When they could not defeat him in debates, they changed their tactics. They hired men to distort Stephen's words. They secretly persuaded some men to say, "We have heard Stephen speak blasphemous words against Moses and against God." They lied about him and charged him with blasphemy, which essentially meant insulting God and His representative, Moses. This is what often happens in the world today. If your opponents can't win a debate against you, they assassinate your character.

The Arrest of Stephen

Verses 12-15: So they stirred up the people and the elders and the teachers of the law. They seized Stephen and brought him before the Sanhedrin. ¹³ *They produced false witnesses, who testified, "This fellow never stops speaking against this holy place and against the law.* ¹⁴ *For we have heard him say that this Jesus of Nazareth will destroy this place and change the customs Moses handed down to us."* ¹⁵ *All who were sitting in the Sanhedrin looked intently at Stephen, and they saw that his face was like the face of an angel.*

12 Based on the false charges against Stephen, they stirred up the people and the elders and the teachers of the law. The crowd was fickle and could be manipulated. They seized Stephen and brought him before the Sanhedrin. When the religious leaders wanted to prosecute the apostles, they did not have the support of the people. With Stephen, the opponents were able to convince the people that he was a blasphemer.

13,14 They produced false witnesses, who testified, "This fellow never stops speaking against this holy place and against the law. For we have heard him say that this Jesus of Nazareth will destroy this place and change the customs Moses handed down to us." The first statement is general; it is explained by the second statement. To the Jews, nothing was more sacred than the temple and nothing was more precious than the law of Moses. The temple was the sanctuary of God's presence and the law was His expressed will.

Jesus never said He would destroy the temple. He only foretold the destruction of the temple (Matthew 24:2). It was no longer necessary to hang onto the shadows of the ceremonies. The reality was Christ and He had come now. As far as we can tell, Stephen taught just what Jesus taught.

15 When the witnesses against Stephen ended speaking, all who were sitting in the Sanhedrin looked intently at Stephen, and they saw that his face was like the face of an angel. His courage sustained him through the ordeal. The presence of the Holy Spirit in Stephen made his face radiate with the glow of God. No one else in history except Moses experienced this (Exodus 34:29, 30). Stephen had been charged with blaspheming Moses, yet God allowed his face to shine like Moses. We next hear Stephen's speech as a message from God.

NOTES

1. John MacArthur, *The MacArthur New Testament Commentary: Acts 1-12* (Chicago, IL: Moody Publishers, 1994), p. 184.
2. Stanley M. Horton, *Acts: a Logion Press Commentary* (Springfield, MO: Logion Press, 2001), p. 138.
3. John MacArthur, p. 188.

Chapter 14

STEPHEN'S DEFENSE - PART 1

Acts 7:1-19

The Call of Abraham

Verses 1-8: Then the high priest asked Stephen, "Are these charges true?" ² To this he replied: "Brothers and fathers, listen to me! The God of glory appeared to our father Abraham while he was still in Mesopotamia, before he lived in Harran. ³ 'Leave your country and your people,' God said, 'and go to the land I will show you.' ⁴ "So he left the land of the Chaldeans and settled in Harran. After the death of his father, God sent him to this land where you are now living. ⁵ He gave him no inheritance here, not even enough ground to set his foot on. But God promised him that he and his descendants after him would possess the land, even though at that time Abraham had no child. ⁶ God spoke to him in this way: 'For four hundred years your descendants will be strangers in a country not their own, and they will be enslaved and mistreated. ⁷ But I will punish the nation they serve as slaves,' God said, 'and afterward they will come out of that country and worship me in this place.' ⁸ Then he gave Abraham the covenant of circumcision. And Abraham became the father of Isaac and circumcised him eight days after his birth. Later Isaac became the father of Jacob, and Jacob became the father of the twelve patriarchs.

1 Then the high priest (possibly Caiaphas, the current high priest, who questioned and condemned Jesus) asked Stephen, "Are these charges true?" His charges were speaking against the temple and against the law. He was also accused of blasphemy, by insulting God and Moses. Stephen did not have to worry what he was going to say. The Holy Spirit would teach him what to say (Luke 12:11, 12). With the help of the Holy Spirit and the OT Scripture, he made a landmark defense.

2 To this he replied by giving a long historical summation, the longest speech in the book of Acts. He said, "Brothers and fathers, listen to me! The God of glory appeared to our father Abraham while he was still in Mesopotamia, before he lived in Harran." He began by referring to them as brothers and fathers. He was one with them in the legacy he shared with them as fellow Jews. He referred to the God of Abraham as the God of glory. He started his address with "the God of glory" and ended it with "the glory of God" (v. 55). He gave the starting point of God's relationship with Israel. It all started when God called Abraham when he was still living in Mesopotamia.

3 "Leave your country and your people," God said, "and go to the land I will show you." Abraham originally grew up in the city of Ur (Genesis 11:31) in the land of the Chaldeans. His relationship with the true God started when God called him. As a man of strong faith, Abraham forsook all (his relatives, friends, countrymen) and followed where God might lead.

4 So Abraham obeyed God and left the land of the Chaldeans and settled in Harran. But Abraham only partially obeyed God. He brought his family with him to Harran. After the death of his father, God sent him to this land where they were now living—Canaan. The fact they were now living in the land of Canaan was a witness to God's faithfulness to their ancestor Abraham.

5 God gave Abraham no inheritance here, not even enough ground to set his foot on. He had no tangible possessions in Canaan. The only small piece of land he had was a burial plot (Genesis 23:9-17). But God promised him that he and his descendants after him would possess the land, even though at that time Abraham had no children. He had only the promise, not the place. He was operating on faith, not by sight. His faith rested on the Word of God.

6 God spoke to him in this way: "For four hundred years your descendants will be strangers in a country not their own, and they will be enslaved and mistreated." Abraham's descendants would settle in Egypt, a foreign land. The exact period that Israelites lived in Egypt was 430 years (Exodus 12:40), but Stephen rounded it as 400. Even Pharaoh, as stubborn and mighty as he was, could not foil God's plan.

7 "But I will punish the nation they serve as slaves," God said, "and afterward they will come out of that country and worship me in this place." God promised to judge the nation that enslaved Abraham's children. This was done when He sent Moses to Pharaoh with the message to "let His people go" and to serve Him "in this place," referring to Mount Horeb. He punished Egypt with plagues for their wickedness against His people. Abraham's descendants would move to the Promised Land after their release from their bondage.

8 Then God gave Abraham the covenant of circumcision. Circumcision was a sign of covenant. It distinguished Jews from Gentiles and the Jews prided themselves in it. And Abraham became the father of Isaac and circumcised him eight days after his birth. Later Isaac became the father of Jacob, and Jacob became the father of the twelve patriarchs. All the descendants of Abraham were born into a covenantal relationship existing between God and His friend Abraham. "God has no grandchildren. Each of us must be born into the family of God through personal faith in Jesus Christ (John 1:11-13)."[1]

Joseph in Egypt

Verses 9-16: "Because the patriarchs were jealous of Joseph, they sold him as a slave into Egypt. But God was with him [10] and rescued him from all his troubles. He gave Joseph wisdom and enabled him to gain the goodwill of Pharaoh king of Egypt. So Pharaoh made him ruler over Egypt and all his palace. [11] "Then a famine struck all Egypt and Canaan, bringing great suffering, and our ancestors could not find food. [12] When Jacob heard that there was grain in Egypt, he sent our forefathers on their first visit. [13] On their second visit, Joseph told his brothers who he was, and Pharaoh learned about Joseph's family. [14] After this, Joseph sent for his father Jacob and his whole family, seventy-five in all. [15] Then Jacob went down to Egypt, where he and our ancestors died. [16] Their bodies were brought back to Shechem and placed in the tomb that Abraham had bought from the sons of Hamor at Shechem for a certain sum of money.

9 Because the patriarchs (the fathers of the Jewish nation) were jealous of Joseph, they sold him as a slave into Egypt. Jacob's ten sons were united to get rid of Joseph. They sold their own brother to foreigners. But God was with him. God allowed all things to work together for good for Joseph (Romans 8:28). Joseph is a great type of Jesus in the OT. Just as the patriarchs rejected Joseph, so the Sanhedrin rejected Jesus for the same reason—jealousy.

10 Joseph went through physical, spiritual, and emotional sufferings. Despite his faithful service to Potiphar, he was treated unfairly at the end. God rescued Joseph from all his troubles. He gave Joseph inspired wisdom and enabled him to gain the favor of Pharaoh, the king of Egypt at that time. In due time, Pharaoh made him ruler over Egypt and all his palace. He became Pharaoh's chief advisor and ruler over all the land.

11 Then a famine struck in Egypt and Canaan, bringing great suffering, and the ancestors could not find food. The famine did not meet the Egyptians by surprise. Joseph had predicted the famine and wisely suggested how to get ready for the famine. The famine reached Canaan, bringing great suffering to Jacob and his sons. God would use Joseph as their source of survival. "The stone the builders rejected has become the capstone" (1 Peter 2:7).

12 When Jacob heard that there was grain in Egypt, he sent our forefathers on their first visit there. "Grain" may mean wheat and barley. People all over the world came to Egypt to buy food, thanks to Joseph's wisdom. The famine was instrumental in sending the forefathers down to Egypt. When the sons of Jacob came to Egypt, Joseph recognized them right away.

13 On their second visit, Joseph told his brothers who he was, and Pharaoh learned about Joseph's family. This opened the door for the entire family of Jacob to move to Egypt. Joseph later told his brothers, "You intended to harm me, but God intended it for good to accomplish what is now being done, the saving of many lives" (Genesis 50:20).

14 Joseph revealed himself to his brothers 22 years after he was sold into slavery. After Joseph's reunion with his brothers, he sent for his father Jacob and his whole family, 75 in all. The discrepancy in the exact number has puzzled some scholars. The number 75 possibly included Joseph's family. Stephen was probably using the Septuagint which states 75 in Genesis 46:27 and Exodus 1:5. The Hebrew text in both verses has 70. This number of 75 does not necessarily contradict any OT text, as some claim.

15 Then Jacob went down to Egypt with his entire family because of the famine. Their rejected brother now became their savior. But Jacob and his sons died there because they were content living there. Jacob lived seventeen more years and died. Jacob (and later Joseph) insisted on being buried in Canaan. Jacob wanted to be buried in the cave of Machpelah where Abraham, Sarah, Isaac, and Rebekah were all buried.

16 Jacob was not buried in Shechem. The bodies of the patriarchs were brought back to Shechem and placed in the tomb that Abraham had bought from the sons of Hamor at Shechem for a certain sum of money. The family tomb was the only portion of the Holy Land that they possessed. Jacob probably repurchased this burial plot.

The Oppression in Egypt

Verses 17-19: "As the time drew near for God to fulfill his promise to Abraham, the number of our people in Egypt had greatly increased. [18] Then 'a new king, to whom Joseph meant nothing, came to power in Egypt.' [19] He dealt treacherously with our people and oppressed our ancestors by forcing them to throw out their newborn babies so that they would die.

17 "As the time drew near for God to fulfill his promise to Abraham, the number of our people in Egypt had greatly" increased. The four hundred years passed quickly. God's promise to Abraham was that He would give the land to him and his offspring. Jacob and his family came to Egypt because of famine. They were content there and did not return to the Promised Land.

18 Then a new king, to whom Joseph meant nothing, came to power in Egypt. The new king did not know Joseph. He was possibly ignorant of the past history. Forgetting the goodness of God only invites trouble. Through hardship, the nation of Israel was "born" and "nurtured" in Egypt. Their number had increase from 75 to one million or more.

19 The new king feared the growing population of Israelites in his country. He was afraid that the Israelites would multiply very fast and rebel against them one day. He dealt treacherously with the people and oppressed the Israelites. He forced them to throw out their newborn babies so that they would die and reduce in number. He also subjected them to hard labor.

NOTES

1. Warren W. Wiersbe, *Be Dynamic: Acts 1-12* (Colorado Springs, CO: David C. Cook, 1987), p. 108.

Chapter 15

STEPHEN'S DEFENSE - PART 2

Acts 7:20-38

The Manifestation of Moses

*Verses 20-29: "At that time Moses was born, and he was no ordinary child.
For three months he was cared for by his family. ²¹ When he was placed
outside, Pharaoh's daughter took him and brought him up as her own son.
²² Moses was educated in all the wisdom of the Egyptians and was powerful
in speech and action. ²³ "When Moses was forty years old, he decided to visit
his own people, the Israelites. ²⁴ He saw one of them being mistreated by an
Egyptian, so he went to his defense and avenged him by killing the Egyptian.
²⁵ Moses thought that his own people would realize that God was using him
to rescue them, but they did not. ²⁶ The next day Moses came upon two
Israelites who were fighting. He tried to reconcile them by saying, 'Men, you
are brothers; why do you want to hurt each other?' ²⁷ "But the man who was
mistreating the other pushed Moses aside and said, 'Who made you ruler and
judge over us? ²⁸ Are you thinking of killing me as you killed the Egyptian
yesterday?'²⁹ When Moses heard this, he fled to Midian, where he settled as a
foreigner and had two sons."*

20 Stephen now turned his focus on discussing Moses, their great hero
and lawgiver. At the time when a king that knew nothing about Joseph
was reigning, Moses was born. It was also a time when Hebrew midwives
were ordered to kill Hebrew boys. God did not choose a more convenient
time for Moses, their God-appointed deliverer, to be born. Moses was
no ordinary child. He was a good-looking child (Exodus 2:2). For three

months he was cared for by his family. Instead of throwing him into the Nile River to drown, the mother of Moses, Jochebed, conceived a plan to rescue her babe.

21 When Moses was placed in a basket in the Nile River, Pharaoh's daughter found and rescued him and brought him up as her own son. She groomed him for the throne. He became Pharaoh's adopted grandson. As the Lord would have it, Jochebed was actually hired to nurse her own son, Moses. Although we do not know how long Moses' mother took care of him, she impressed on him the fact that he was a Hebrew.

22 Moses was educated in all the wisdom of the Egyptians and was powerful in speech and action. He had the most comprehensive education of the land. He increased in wisdom and in stature. He had at his disposal the luxuries, wealth, and privileges of Egypt. Out of God was preparing him for the task ahead. He would be the vehicle God would use to deliver His people.

23 When Moses was forty years old, he decided to visit his own people, the Israelites. He wanted to investigate their situation and try to remedy it. Moses had not forgotten his own people despite the fact that he was raised in the Egyptian palace. He identified himself with his oppressed people. He visited them to deliver them from Egyptian bondage and oppression, but they did not understand his intentions or accept him as their deliverer or savior.

24 Stephen presents Moses' first attempt to deliver his people. He saw one of them being mistreated by an Egyptian, so he went to his defense and avenged him by killing the Egyptian. Moses jumped ahead of God and attempted to do in the flesh what God had plans to do in the Spirit. He was disappointed. He later realized it was not yet time to deliver Israel from oppression.

25 Moses thought that his own people would realize that God was using him to rescue them, but they did not. They rejected him as their deliverer, just as they rejected Christ. Their stubbornness would prevent them from leaving Egypt forty years before they actually did. Because of their rejection, they remained in Egypt for another forty years of slavery.

26 The next day Moses came upon two Israelites who were fighting. As a peacemaker, Moses tried to reconcile them by saying, "Men, you are brothers; why do you want to hurt each other?" It is foolish for brothers to fight against each other. Moses attempted to establish peace between the fighting Jews, but they failed to understand his intentions.

27,28 But the man who was mistreating the other pushed Moses aside and said, "Who made you ruler and judge over us? Are you thinking of killing me as you killed the Egyptian yesterday?" The man questioned Moses as he tried to intercede in their quarrel. He did not know that God had appointed Moses as ruler and judge of Israel. He did not see the need for Moses' ministry of reconciliation. He misunderstood Moses. He thought Moses was using his powerful political position to lord over them. So Moses was rejected.

29 When Moses heard this, he realized that his killing of the Egyptian yesterday was widely known by now. What he did in secret was already common knowledge. To escape any retribution, he fled from Egypt, leaving behind all the comfort and luxuries. He fled to Midian, where he settled as a foreigner. He married the daughter of Jethro and had two sons. His mode of living changed. His home was now far away in a different land. He was now a shepherd, not a prince.

God Speaks to Moses

Verses 30-34: "After forty years had passed, an angel appeared to Moses in the flames of a burning bush in the desert near Mount Sinai. [31] When he saw this, he was amazed at the sight. As he went over to get a closer look, he heard the Lord say: [32] 'I am the God of your fathers, the God of Abraham, Isaac and Jacob.' Moses trembled with fear and did not dare to look. [33] "Then the Lord said to him, 'Take off your sandals, for the place where you are standing is holy ground. [34] I have indeed seen the oppression of my people in Egypt. I have heard their groaning and have come down to set them free. Now come, I will send you back to Egypt.'"

30 After forty years had passed (Moses was now eighty years old), an angel appeared to Moses in the flames of a burning bush in the desert near Mount Sinai. It was an incredible moment as Moses saw God work and speak. Moses was tending sheep in the desert when the Lord appeared to him. God had used the previous forty years to prepare Moses for the task and to prepare the Israelites for Moses' leadership.

31,32 When Moses saw the flame of fire burning and the bush was not consumed, he was amazed at the sight. As he went over to get a closer look, he heard the Lord say: "I am the God of your fathers, the God of Abraham, Isaac and Jacob." The angel said He was the Lord, a covenant-keeping God. Referring to Abraham, Isaac, and Jacob would connect the past revelation to the patriarchs with the present revelation to Moses.

As one would expect, Moses trembled with fear and did not dare to look. "This fear that Moses had was good and healthy and ought to characterize our relationship with the Lord."[1]

33 Then the Lord said to him, "Take off your sandals, for the place where you are standing is holy ground." Moses was asked to remove his sandals because he was standing on holy ground (Exodus 3:5). This piece of land in Sinai was regarded as holy because God was revealing Himself there. The Jews Stephen was addressing believed that the temple was a holy place because God resided there.

34 "I have indeed seen the oppression of my people in Egypt. I have heard their groaning and have come down to set them free. Now come, I will send you back to Egypt." With time, the oppression of the Hebrews in Egypt grew worse. The people cried out to God and He heard their groaning. He came down from heaven to set them free. He would not be doing the deliverance alone. He would use Moses.

Moses Leads Israel Out of Egypt

Verses 35-38: "This is the same Moses they had rejected with the words, 'Who made you ruler and judge?' He was sent to be their ruler and deliverer by God himself, through the angel who appeared to him in the bush. ³⁶ He led them out of Egypt and performed wonders and signs in Egypt, at the Red Sea and for forty years in the wilderness. ³⁷ "This is the Moses who told the Israelites, 'God will raise up for you a prophet like me from your own people.' ³⁸ He was in the assembly in the wilderness, with the angel who spoke to him on Mount Sinai, and with our ancestors; and he received living words to pass on to us.

35 This is the same Moses they had rejected with the words, "Who made you ruler and judge?" He was sent to be their ruler and deliverer by God Himself, through the angel who appeared to him in the bush. Moses started to act as God's deliverer. Initially, they did not recognize him as such. God reassured Moses that He Himself appointed him as ruler of His people.

36 He led them out of Egypt and performed wonders and signs in Egypt, at the Red Sea and for forty years in the wilderness. These wonders and signs were monumental in Israel's history. Israel was redeemed and set free by God's mighty hand. God judged Egypt and set Israel apart to start a new life, a life that witnessed miracle after miracle.

37 This is the Moses who told the Israelites, "God will raise up for you a prophet like me from your own people." This is taken from Deuteronomy 18:16. There Moses predicted that a prophet like him would be raised up. The Jews were looking for him as the ultimate prophet. God primarily made His will known to Israel through the prophets. "Surely the Sovereign LORD does nothing without revealing his plan to his servants the prophets" (Amos 3:7). Jesus is the one prophesied about by Moses.

38 He was in the assembly in the wilderness, with the angel who spoke to him on Mount Sinai, and with our ancestors; and he received living words to pass on to us. The word "assembly" means "called out ones." It is the same word used for "church." God powerfully called the Israelites out of Egypt to serve Him. Israel was God's church in the wilderness. Moses received the living words from God and was commissioned to pass them on to the people.

NOTES

1. Derek Carlsen, *Faith & Courage: Commentary on Acts* (Arlington Heights, IL: Christian Liberty Press, 2000), p. 173.

Chapter 16

STEPHEN'S DEFENSE - PART 3

Acts 7:39-60

The Idolatry of Israel

Verses 39-43: "But our ancestors refused to obey him. Instead, they rejected him and in their hearts turned back to Egypt. ⁴⁰ They told Aaron, 'Make us gods who will go before us. As for this fellow Moses who led us out of Egypt— we don't know what has happened to him!' ⁴¹ That was the time they made an idol in the form of a calf. They brought sacrifices to it and reveled in what their own hands had made. ⁴² But God turned away from them and gave them over to the worship of the sun, moon and stars. This agrees with what is written in the book of the prophets:

Did you bring me sacrifices and offerings
forty years in the wilderness, people of Israel?
⁴³ You have taken up the tabernacle of Molek
*   and the star of your god Rephan,*
*   the idols you made to worship.*
*   Therefore I will send you into exile beyond Babylon.*

39 Stephen mentioned that their ancestors refused to obey Moses. They told Moses, "You tell us what God says and we will listen." But they did not listen. They did not obey Moses and the law he mediated. Instead of obeying Moses, they rejected him—his leadership, his message, and his claim as God's spokesman. This was the second and worst rejection of Moses, a rejection of God. In their hearts they turned back to Egypt.

81

They felt it was better for them to be slaves in Egypt than to be the Lord's freemen. They forgot the amazing signs and wonders they had witnessed.

40 Moses had ascended the mountain to receive the commandments from God. The people were impatient. They got tired of waiting. They felt Moses had died in God's terrifying presence. They told Aaron, "Make us gods who will go before us. As for this fellow Moses who led us out of Egypt—we don't know what has happened to him!" They were used to worshipping idols in Egypt. After they settled in Canaan, they adopted the gods of the nations around them.

41 That was the time they made an idol in the form of a calf. They brought sacrifices to it and reveled in what their own hands had made. The people got the idea of calf worship from Egypt. They had persisted in superstition, rebellion, and idol worship. The invisible God and "absent" leader Moses were too much for them to bear. They preferred something they would see with their naked eyes. This was the beginning of a significant downward spiral for them.

42,43 God turned away from them and gave them over to the worship of the sun, moon and stars. This agrees with what is written in the book of the prophets: "Did you bring me sacrifices and offerings forty years in the wilderness, people of Israel? You have taken up the tabernacle of Molek and the star of your god Rephan, the idols you made to worship. Therefore I will send you into exile beyond Babylon." This is quoted from Amos 5:25-27 except that Amos used Damascus while Stephen used Babylon.

God repeatedly warned the people by sending prophet after prophet, but they would not listen. He allowed them to be taken captive to Babylon. He became their enemy. Such a sad situation did not happen in an instant. Stephen was able to show that Israel's idolatry began in the wilderness and continued to the Babylonian exile.

The Tabernacle/Temple

Verses 44-50: "Our ancestors had the tabernacle of the covenant law with them in the wilderness. It had been made as God directed Moses, according to the pattern he had seen. ⁴⁵ After receiving the tabernacle, our ancestors

under Joshua brought it with them when they took the land from the nations
God drove out before them. It remained in the land until the time of David,
⁴⁶ who enjoyed God's favor and asked that he might provide a dwelling place
for the God of Jacob. ⁴⁷ But it was Solomon who built a house for him.
⁴⁸However, the Most High does not live in houses made by human hands. As
the prophet says:

⁴⁹ 'Heaven is my throne,
  and the earth is my footstool.
  What kind of house will you build for me?
  says the Lord.
  Or where will my resting place be?
⁵⁰ Has not my hand made all these things?'

44 Starting with the tabernacle, Stephen traced the history of the temple.
Their ancestors had the tabernacle of the covenant law with them in the
wilderness. It had been made as God directed Moses, according to the
pattern he had seen. The tent was built to divine specification. It was a
portable worship structure. They saw the glory of God dwelling in the
tabernacle as they journeyed through the wilderness.

45 After receiving the tabernacle, their ancestors under Joshua's
leadership brought it with them when they took the land from the nations
God drove out before them. It remained in the land until the time of
David. It was carried from place to place showing that God is a pilgrim
God. From the time they entered the Promised Land under the leadership
of Joshua until the time of King David, the tabernacle was with them,
reminding them of God's holy presence.

46 King David enjoyed God's favor and asked that he might provide a
dwelling place for the God of Jacob. David's strong desire is expressed in
the Psalm: "I couldn't rest, I couldn't sleep, thinking how I ought to build
a permanent home for the Ark of the Lord, a Temple for the mighty one
of Israel. Then I vowed that I would do it; I made a solemn promise to the
Lord" (Psalm 132:2-5, TLB). But God would not allow David to build
Him a dwelling place because he was a man of blood. Nevertheless, God
would allow David's son to build a house for God (2 Samuel 7:12-14).

47 It was Solomon, David's son, who built a temple for God in Jerusalem using the materials his father had provided. God permitted Solomon, a man of peace, to build the magnificent temple according to His promise to David. "The current temple was not Solomon's, which had been destroyed by the Babylonians (Ezra 5:12). That temple had been replaced by one built by Zerubbabel (Ezra 5:2), which had also been destroyed. The current temple had been built by the non-Jew Herod."[1]

48-50 However, the Most High does not live in houses made by human hands. As the prophet says: "Heaven is my throne, and the earth is my footstool. What kind of house will you build for me? says the Lord. Or where will my resting place be? Has not my hand made all these things?" Stephen quoted Isaiah 66:1,2 on the inadequacy of the temple.

The omnipresent God cannot be confined to a place and He does not need a man-made temple. When Solomon was dedicating the temple he built for the Lord, he openly declared, "But will God really dwell on earth with men? The heavens, even the highest heavens, cannot contain you. How much less this temple I have built" (2 Chronicles 6:18). Jeremiah warned the people about their superstitious faith in the temple or house of God (Jeremiah 7:9-16). So Stephen was saying that the people should not trust God's house more than they trust God Himself.

Stephen's Accusation

Verses 51-53: "You stiff-necked people! Your hearts and ears are still uncircumcised. You are just like your ancestors: You always resist the Holy Spirit! [52] *Was there ever a prophet your ancestors did not persecute? They even killed those who predicted the coming of the Righteous One. And now you have betrayed and murdered him—* [53] *you who have received the law that was given through angels but have not obeyed it."*

51 Stephen had proven his case. He now boldly attacked and accused his listeners of three things. First, they were stiff-necked or stubborn people (Exodus 33:3). They continued to suppress the light of God and refused to turn back to God. Second, their hearts and ears were still uncircumcised. They were like the Gentiles. They were not willing to obey with their heart or hear with their ears. Third, they were just like their ancestors who always resisted the Holy Spirit. The Holy Spirit can be grieved and quenched. Their rejection of Christ was not due to ignorance but to a deliberate resistance to the Holy Spirit.

52 Was there ever a prophet their ancestors did not persecute? Stephen challenged them to name a prophet their ancestors did not persecute. They stoned some and imprisoned others. They even killed those who predicted the coming of the Righteous One. They went on to betray and murder Him. They had murdered God's Son and thus destroyed the source of hope and life.

53 Although they prided themselves on receiving the law that was given through angels, they had not obeyed it. Israel's whole history had been that of breaking the law. To receive God's revelation was a great privilege and wonderful blessing. They had God's standard of right and wrong. But what is the use of the revelation when they disobey it?

Stephen is Stoned

Verses 54-60: *When the members of the Sanhedrin heard this, they were furious and gnashed their teeth at him. ⁵⁵ But Stephen, full of the Holy Spirit, looked up to heaven and saw the glory of God, and Jesus standing at the right hand of God. ⁵⁶ "Look," he said, "I see heaven open and the Son of Man standing at the right hand of God." ⁵⁷ At this they covered their ears and, yelling at the top of their voices, they all rushed at him, ⁵⁸ dragged him out of the city and began to stone him. Meanwhile, the witnesses laid their coats at the feet of a young man named Saul. ⁵⁹ While they were stoning him, Stephen prayed, "Lord Jesus, receive my spirit." ⁶⁰ Then he fell on his knees and cried out, "Lord, do not hold this sin against them." When he had said this, he fell asleep.*

54 When the members of the Sanhedrin heard this, their reaction was bitter as one would expect. They were furious and gnashed their teeth at him. What Stephen said caused the religious leaders to be infuriated instead of repenting. The Sanhedrin had heard the truth from Jesus before and now from Stephen. Stephen now gave an indictment rather than an invitation. Through the power of the Holy Spirit, they were cut to the heart. Guilt is a terrible thing to carry. One must repent and have faith in Christ's work of atonement.

55 But Stephen did not care about their reaction. In contrast to these religious leaders who resisted the Holy Spirit and were now gnashing their teeth, Stephen had a vision of heaven. Being full of the Holy Spirit, he looked up to heaven and saw the glory of God, and Jesus standing at the right hand of God. The Holy Spirit provided special grace and encouragement for Stephen. Spirit-filled preaching always produces strong conviction in the listeners.

56 "Look," he said, "I see heaven open and the Son of Man standing at the right hand of God." The title "Son of Man" was used by Jesus to refer to Himself. The picture of Jesus being at the right hand of God alludes to Psalm 110:1. Jesus is often described as seated at God's right hand (e.g. Luke 22:69) because He has completed the work of redemption, but here He stood up because of Stephen. As John MacArthur rightly observed, "Stephen was one of the few in Scripture blessed with a glimpse into heaven, along with Isaiah (Isa. 6:1-3), Ezekiel (Ezek. 1:26-28), Paul (2 Cor. 12:2-4), and John (Rev. 4:1ff.)."[2]

57 The religious leaders stopped up their ears. They covered their ears because they did not want to hear the blasphemous words coming out of Stephen's mouth. They had heard enough from him. As the proverb says, "There are none so deaf as those who will not hear." Stephen was right there when he said that their "ears" were "uncircumcised." They yelled at the top of their voices. With mob violence, they all rushed at him.

58 They dragged him out of the city and began to stone him. They followed Leviticus 24:13-17, which specifies that a blasphemer should be stoned outside the camp. The witnesses were required to be the first to stone the condemned person (Deuteronomy 17:7). Meanwhile, the witnesses laid their coats at the feet of a young man named Saul. This is our first introduction to the man Saul. He was a zealous Pharisee. He came from Tarsus in Cilicia and would later be known as Paul the apostle.

59 While they were stoning him, Stephen prayed, "Lord Jesus, receive my spirit." Just as Jesus committed His spirit to His Father (Luke 23:46), Stephen committed his spirit to Jesus. Stephen believed that he would enter Christ's presence right after death. No time for purgatory or soul-sleep. "Just as man is destined to die once, and after that to face judgment" (Hebrew 9:27).

60 Then Stephen fell on his knees and cried out, "Lord, do not hold this sin against them." He was on the verge of leaving this life. In spite of enduring physical suffering from stoning, he pleaded for their forgiveness. Although God may not call of us to die for Him, He does call all of us to serve Him. When he had said this, he fell asleep. When believers die, they fall asleep. That is the end of their life. They go on to live with Christ. Stephen became the first martyr of the church to die for Jesus.

NOTES

1. John MacArthur, *The MacArthur New Testament Commentary: Acts 1-12* (Chicago, IL: Moody Publishers, 1994), p. 214.
2. Ibid., p. 222.

Chapter 17

THE WITNESS OF PHILIP - PART 1

Acts 8:1-25

The Church Persecuted

Verses 1-3: And Saul approved of their killing him. On that day a great persecution broke out against the church in Jerusalem, and all except the apostles were scattered throughout Judea and Samaria. ² Godly men buried Stephen and mourned deeply for him. ³ But Saul began to destroy the church. Going from house to house, he dragged off both men and women and put them in prison.

1 Saul approved of and participated in the killing of Stephen. This is the first mention of Saul, named after King Saul, the first king of Israel. He was from the tribe of Benjamin.

On the day that Stephen was stoned to death, a great persecution broke out against the church in Jerusalem. Initially, only the apostles and their associates were persecuted. Now the persecution was directed toward the whole church. Stephen's death served as a catalyst for the brutal persecution of the Jerusalem church. His death had two immediate consequences. First, Stephen's death provoked a great persecution of the church. The campaign of intolerance and terror was led by Saul. Second, all believers except the apostles were scattered throughout Judea and Samaria. The apostles remained in Jerusalem since Jerusalem was still a mission field.

2 Godly men buried Stephen and mourned deeply for him. The church had lost a champion. Devout men of the church buried Stephen with dignity and lamented over his death. There was really no need to mourn for Stephen since he was alive and well in the presence of the Lord. Stephen happened to be the first Christian martyr. Thousands of believers would follow in his footsteps and give their lives for the sake of Christ. As someone has said, "The blood of the martyrs is the seed of the church."

3 The storm of persecution continued. Saul began to destroy the church. He "made havoc of the church" (KJV). His zeal for the law motivated him to persecute the church (Galatians 1:13, 14; Philippians 3:6). Going from house to house looking for Christians, he dragged off both men and women and put them in prison. With permission from the religious leaders, he pursued them to foreign cities. By persecuting Christians, he thought he was serving God.

Samaritan Salvation

Verses 4-8: Those who had been scattered preached the word wherever they went. ⁵ Philip went down to a city in Samaria and proclaimed the Messiah there. ⁶ When the crowds heard Philip and saw the signs he performed, they all paid close attention to what he said. ⁷ For with shrieks, impure spirits came out of many, and many who were paralyzed or lame were healed. ⁸ So there was great joy in that city.

4 Despite the persecution, those who had been scattered preached the word wherever they went. The persecution never stopped the spread of the gospel; it had the opposite effect. Although they were persecuted and scattered, they could not be silent. Their faith was with them. They were motivated to preach the Word. Till now, the message of salvation was confined to Jerusalem and Judea. The scattering allowed the message to reach other places. The message was not just for the Jews but for all people.

5 Philip went down to a city in Samaria and proclaimed the Messiah there. (Some versions name the city as Samaria.) This Philip was not one of the twelve apostles but one of the seven men chosen to serve the needs of the widows. Philip and Stephen were among the seven "deacons." "One became the first great martyr of the faith; another became the first great missionary of the faith."[1] God uses ordinary people to accomplish His purposes.

Samaria was a province north of Judea. "Israel had been divided into three main regions—Galilee in the north, Samaria in the middle, and Judea in the south."[2] As a region, Samaria had a number of cities. The Jews regarded the Samaritans as defecting half-breeds (a mixture of Jew and Gentile) and refused to have any dealing with them. The Samaritans worshiped Israel's God and observed the laws of Moses. In spite of the hostility between the Jews and the Samaritans (e.g. John 4:9), Philip went to one of their cities to preach the gospel.

6 When the crowds, which included all classes of people, heard Philip and saw the signs he performed, they all paid close attention to what he said. The signs Philip performed authenticated the message and the messenger. They also got the attention of the crowds. This confirms what Jesus said in Mark 16:17, 18 that some signs will accompany those who believe. Jesus Christ is the same yesterday, today, and forever.

7 This verse provides some examples of the signs performed by Philip. Impure spirits came out of many, "screaming as they left their victims" (TLB). Many who were paralyzed or lame were healed. Some claim that sign gifts no longer operate in the church today. But there is no Scripture to support this. As they did in the case of Philip and others in the NT, the sign gifts make the power of God evident.

8 So there was great joy in that city. As a result of Philip's preaching and healing ministry, many Samaritans believed and were saved. When people get right with God and with one another, such a revival produces great rejoicing. The prodigal had returned and the Lord must celebrate it. They rejoiced over God's power. The entire city changed as deep joy filled the hearts of believers there.

Simon the Sorcerer

Verses 9-13: Now for some time a man named Simon had practiced sorcery in the city and amazed all the people of Samaria. He boasted that he was someone great, [10] and all the people, both high and low, gave him their attention and exclaimed, "This man is rightly called the Great Power of

God." [11] They followed him because he had amazed them for a long time with his sorcery. [12] But when they believed Philip as he proclaimed the good news of the kingdom of God and the name of Jesus Christ, they were baptized, both men and women. [13] Simon himself believed and was baptized. And he followed Philip everywhere, astonished by the great signs and miracles he saw.

9 Among Philip's listeners, Luke pays special attention to one Simon. For some time a man named Simon had practiced sorcery in the city. He was able to amaze all the people of Samaria. He boasted that he was someone great and many people believed him. He operated in the supernatural using demonic powers. There was a legendary man named Simon Magus who might have been this Simon. The word "Magus" is not used here by Luke but is of later tradition.

10 All the people in Samaria, both high and low, gave him their attention and exclaimed, "This man is rightly called the Great Power of God." People spoke highly of Simon and were impressed by his magical power. Simon claimed to possess the power of God. As always, this pride would lead to his fall. Pride is thinking of oneself more highly than one ought. It is boasting in one's ability as if it were not a gift from God (1 Corinthians 4:7).

11 They followed him because he had amazed them for a long time with his sorcery. He was able to deceive a lot of people through his sorcery. He had demonic power to do mighty things. However, the evil spirit that energized Simon recognized the superior power that energized Philip. Luke presents Simon as a magician who deceived and manipulated the people by his tricks.

12 Simon's sorcery could not contend with Philip's Spirit-given power. When they believed Philip as he proclaimed the good news of the kingdom of God and the name of Jesus Christ, they were baptized, both men and women. Baptism served as the ritual of incorporation into the new community of faith. As people believed and joined the body of Christ, Simon saw his influence diminishing. They paid attention to Philip instead of to Simon.

13 Simon himself "believed" and was baptized. He actually pretended to be a converted follower. The external act of baptism could not transform his life or save his soul. He followed Philip everywhere, astonished by the great signs and miracles he saw. As they say, "If you can't beat them, join them." But the genuineness of his conversion is questionable.

Samaritans Receive the Holy Spirit

Verses 14-17: When the apostles in Jerusalem heard that Samaria had accepted the word of God, they sent Peter and John to Samaria. ¹⁵ When they arrived, they prayed for the new believers there that they might receive the Holy Spirit, ¹⁶ because the Holy Spirit had not yet come on any of them; they had simply been baptized in the name of the Lord Jesus. ¹⁷ Then Peter and John placed their hands on them, and they received the Holy Spirit.

14 When the apostles in Jerusalem heard that many in Samaria had accepted the word of God, they sent Peter and John there. That the so-called half-breeds had been added to the kingdom of God was shocking news to the apostles in Jerusalem. They sent a delegation, Peter and John, to check it out. It was John who asked the Lord if they should call down fire from heaven to burn a Samaritan village that did not welcome them (Luke 9:51-55).

15,16 When they arrived, they prayed for the new believers there that they might receive the Holy Spirit, because the Holy Spirit had not yet come on any of them; they had simply been baptized in the name of the Lord Jesus. Some see this as a clear example of people who were saved but had not been baptized with the Holy Spirit.

Every believer, then and now, receives the Holy Spirit when one is saved. One may or may not receive the baptism of the Holy Spirit at salvation. Apparently, the Samaritan Christians did not receive the Holy Spirit baptism at salvation. The baptism is the fullness of the Spirit. Even the apostles too were saved and had the Holy Spirit before Pentecost. It was at Pentecost, however, that they received the baptism of the Holy Spirit. This is what some now call the two-stage experience of conversion/baptism of the Holy Spirit. We must resist the temptation of interpreting the Scriptures in the light of our own experience.

17 Then Peter and John placed their hands on the new believers, and they received the Holy Spirit. They believed that it was important for the Samaritans to have the Holy Spirit baptism. The two apostles were not just there to welcome the Samaritans into the body of Christ, but to impart the Spirit on them through the laying on of hands. Apparently, Philip did not have the gift of laying hands on people to receive the Spirit. He had to wait for Peter and John who had this gift.

Simon's Simony

Verses 18-25: When Simon saw that the Spirit was given at the laying on of the apostles' hands, he offered them money [19] *and said, "Give me also this ability so that everyone on whom I lay my hands may receive the Holy Spirit."* [20] *Peter answered: "May your money perish with you, because you thought you could buy the gift of God with money!* [21] *You have no part or share in this ministry, because your heart is not right before God.* [22] *Repent of this wickedness and pray to the Lord in the hope that he may forgive you for having such a thought in your heart.* [23] *For I see that you are full of bitterness and captive to sin."* [24] *Then Simon answered, "Pray to the Lord for me so that nothing you have said may happen to me."* [25] *After they had further proclaimed the word of the Lord and testified about Jesus, Peter and John returned to Jerusalem, preaching the gospel in many Samaritan villages.*

18 When Simon saw that the Spirit was given at the laying on of the apostles' hands, he offered them money. To him, it was an irresistible display of power. He was greatly impressed by Peter and John. He wanted what they had—the ability to lay hands on people with the same results. He desired to have the same kind of power and prestige. He thought he could buy such authority with money. In his world, everything had a price tag. He wanted power and would pay anything for it. He offered the apostles cash if they would give him what they had.

19 Simon expressed his greed in words. He said to the apostles, "Give me also this ability so that everyone on whom I lay my hands may receive the Holy Spirit." He was willing to purchase the secret of their power. He expressed his ignorance by thinking that money could buy God's gift. It is from this act that the term "simony" comes from. It refers to the buying and selling of spiritual office and benefits within the church. Some people believe that they can buy God's gifts, salvation, favor or healing.

20 Peter answered: "May your money perish with you, because you thought you could buy the gift of God with money!" J.B. Phillips translated Peter's statement as "To hell with you and your money!" There are many things money cannot buy and the Holy Spirit is one of them. The gifts of the Spirit come from God—free and freely given. They are not for personal gain. They are for the edification of the body of Christ and for exalting God's name.

21 "You have no part or share in this ministry, because your heart is not right before God." Peter rebuked Simon and pronounced judgment on him. Simon had spoken out of the overflow of his heart (Luke 6:45). What he said showed that his heart was not right before God. He was seeking crooked and perverse ways. His offer was offensive to Peter and God. He was probably not converted or saved.

22 Peter followed his rebuke with a call for repentance. He said, "Repent of this wickedness and pray to the Lord in the hope that he may forgive you for having such a thought in your heart." The wickedness Simon needed to repent of was thinking that he could purchase God's power with his money. As a soul-winner, Peter urged Simon to repent and pray for forgiveness. The truly repentant seek forgiveness by surrendering themselves to God's mercy.

23 "For I see that you are full of bitterness and captive to sin." Simon had pretended to be a born-again believer. Though he could fool other believers, he could not deceive the Holy Spirit. Peter discerned Simon's heart, which was full of bitterness. Simon's being was completely enslaved to wickedness, yielding gall of bitterness. He was warned that unless he repented, a chain of sin would enslave him. This was a dangerous condition.

24 Then Simon answered, "Pray to the Lord for me so that nothing you have said may happen to me." He did not repent or ask the Lord for forgiveness. Tradition holds that Simon was the source of many heresies. He was only concerned that nothing Peter said would happen to him.

Like Simon, many people would like to escape the consequences of their sin but are not willing to part with their sin.

25 After they had further proclaimed the word of the Lord and testified about Jesus, Peter and John returned to Jerusalem. On their way, they preached the gospel in many Samaritan villages. They lost no opportunity to share the gospel with others. "Thus the third phase of world evangelism was accomplished. Jerusalem, Judea, and Samaria had heard the Gospel. The stage has now to be set to evangelize 'the uttermost parts of the earth.'"[3] Like the apostles, it is our responsibility to share the good news wherever we go.

NOTES

1. John Phillips, *Exploring Acts* (Grand Rapids, MI: Kregel Publications, 1986), p. 148.
2. Bruce B. Barton et al., *Life Application Bible Commentary: Acts* (Carol Stream, IL: Tyndale House Publishers, 1999), p. 135.
3. John Phillips, p. 158.

Chapter 18

THE WITNESS OF PHILIP - PART 2

Acts 8:26-40

Philip Asked to Join the Ethiopian Eunuch

Verses 26-29: Now an angel of the Lord said to Philip, "Go south to the road—the desert road—that goes down from Jerusalem to Gaza." ²⁷ So he started out, and on his way he met an Ethiopian eunuch, an important official in charge of all the treasury of the Kandake (which means "queen of the Ethiopians"). This man had gone to Jerusalem to worship, ²⁸ and on his way home was sitting in his chariot reading the Book of Isaiah the prophet. ²⁹ The Spirit told Philip, "Go to that chariot and stay near it."

26 While Philip was busy ministering in Samaria, an angel of the Lord said to him, "Go south to the road—the desert road—that goes down from Jerusalem to Gaza." There were two roads that linked the cities Jerusalem and Gaza; Philip took the less used one. Gaza was the most southern of the five popular cities of the Philistines, along with Gath, Ekron, Ashdod, and Ashkelon.

The events that eventually led to the salvation of the Ethiopian eunuch were orchestrated by the Lord's Spirit. A human instrument was involved as usual. God could have used the angel to tell the eunuch about salvation, but He has not given angels such a commission. It is the duty of every Christian to boldly share the gospel with others as the Lord leads.

27 Philip was prepared to serve anywhere anytime. He promptly obeyed the angel and started out. On his way he met an Ethiopian eunuch, an important official in charge of all the treasury of the Kandake (which means "queen of the Ethiopians"). The term "eunuch" means that the man had been castrated. This man had gone to Jerusalem to worship and was returning home. He was a black man and a proselyte to Judaism. He had unsatisfied hunger in his heart. He was a sincere seeker of the true God, as evident by the long journey from his homeland to Jerusalem. Back then Ethiopia was a kingdom south of Egypt.

28 The Ethiopian eunuch was returning home by way of Egypt. On his way, he was sitting in his chariot reading the Book of Isaiah the prophet. Like having a car today, only the most well-to-do had chariots back then. He probably purchased the scrolls of Isaiah while in Jerusalem. He was reading the Scripture to know more about God and desiring to understand it. Faith comes by hearing the Word of God (Romans 10:17, KJV).

29 The Holy Spirit guided Philip and told him, "Go to that chariot and stay near it." By staying near the chariot, Philip could hear what the eunuch was reading since it was customary to read aloud in those days. Philip was prepared and directed by the Holy Spirit to witness to the person riding on the chariot. God noticed the eunuch with a hungry heart and sent Philip to show him the way of salvation. One person is important in the eyes of God. He values one individual as much as the multitudes.

Philip Explains the Scripture to the Eunuch

Verses 30-35: Then Philip ran up to the chariot and heard the man reading Isaiah the prophet. "Do you understand what you are reading?" Philip asked.[31] "How can I," he said, "unless someone explains it to me?" So he invited Philip to come up and sit with him. [32] This is the passage of Scripture the eunuch was reading: "He was led like a sheep to the slaughter, and as a lamb before its shearer is silent, so he did not open his mouth.[33] In his humiliation he was deprived of justice. Who can speak of his descendants? For his life was taken from the earth."[34] The eunuch asked Philip, "Tell me, please, who is the prophet talking about, himself or someone else?" [35] Then Philip began with that very passage of Scripture and told him the good news about Jesus.

30 There are differences between Philip and the eunuch and Philip could have used them as excuses not to approach the man. But Philip ran up to the chariot to be there at the right time when the eunuch would be reading Isaiah 53. He heard the man reading Isaiah the prophet. "Do you understand what you are reading?" Philip asked. The evangelist's question referred to the meaning of what the eunuch was reading.

31 The eunuch's counter-question: "How can I," he said, "unless someone explains it to me?" This question is the main reason we have seminaries and Bible colleges today. In humility the eunuch admitted a lack of understanding. So he invited Philip to come up and sit with him. Today we need teachers to teach the Word of God and make it simple and clear. Teachers along with pastors are real gifts from God (Ephesians 4:11-14).

32,33 In the providence of God, the eunuch was reading writings of the prophet Isaiah. This is the passage of Scripture the eunuch was reading: "He was led like a sheep to the slaughter, and as a lamb before its shearer is silent, so he did not open his mouth. In his humiliation he was deprived of justice. Who can speak of his descendants? For his life was taken from the earth." This passage is from Isaiah 53:7, 8. It was the prophecy of God's suffering servant—His unjust humiliation and sufferings. He suffered for sinners to the point of forfeiting His own human rights. He made no protest when humiliated and deprived of justice. He was eventually put to death. But He then arose and was exalted. This passage provided a great opportunity for the evangelist to explain Christ.

34 The passage perplexed the eunuch. He asked Philip, "Tell me, please, who is the prophet talking about, himself or someone else?" Scholars have suggested that the prophet was referring to himself or the nation or the Messiah. Philip was able to relate the Isaiah passage to the Messiah. He showed that the passage referred to the Messiah and that the Messiah was Jesus.

35 The evangelist had a good text and an anxious listener. He began with that very passage of Scripture and told the eunuch the Good News about Jesus. He started where the eunuch was scripturally and share the gospel message with him. He led him to the Savior. Like Philip, we must not be too busy to listen and adapt our message to the needs of others.

The Eunuch is Baptized

Verses 36-40: As they traveled along the road, they came to some water and the eunuch said, "Look, here is water. What can stand in the way of my being baptized?" [37] 38 And he gave orders to stop the chariot. Then both Philip and the eunuch went down into the water and Philip baptized him. 39 When they came up out of the water, the Spirit of the Lord suddenly took Philip away, and the eunuch did not see him again, but went on his way rejoicing. 40 Philip, however, appeared at Azotus and traveled about, preaching the gospel in all the towns until he reached Caesarea.

36 As they traveled along the road, they came to some water and the eunuch said, "Look, here is water. What can stand in the way of my being baptized?" The eunuch must have heard from Philip about the need for baptism and a public confession of Christ. When the right moment came, he wanted to be baptized and Philip agreed.

37 Most reliable manuscripts do not have verse 37. Most critics argue that the verse should not be in the Bible.

38 The eunuch gave orders to stop the chariot indicating he had a driver and probably an entourage. To fulfill all righteousness, he did what was commanded. Then both Philip and the eunuch went down into the water and Philip baptized him. The baptism was by full immersion. Through baptism we publicly identify with Christ and confess Him as our Lord and Savior. Baptism must be the first acts of new converts.

39 When they came up out of the water, the Spirit of the Lord suddenly took Philip away. The eunuch did not see him again, but went on his way rejoicing. Joy is the outcome of a genuine conversion. The eunuch was happy because he had found in Jesus what he could not find in Judaism. To be taken or caught away refers to being supernaturally taken away when one's assignment is complete. Some see this as "a supersonic ride." Elijah (2 Kings 2:11) and Ezekiel (Ezekiel 3:12) were also snatched away.

Dr. Matthew N. O. Sadiku

This is an abrupt end to the story. The evangelist had completed his job and had moved on as the Spirit leads.

40 Philip, however, later appeared at Azotus, twenty miles north of Gaza. Azotus is the modern-day replacement of the old Philistine city Ashod. He traveled about, preaching the gospel in all the towns until he reached Caesarea. It seems that the evangelist settled down in Caesarea. The next time we see him, he was a family man with four unmarried daughters who were prophetesses (Acts 21:8, 9).

Chapter 19

THE CALL OF SAUL

Acts 9:1-19

The Conversion of Saul

Verses 1-9: Meanwhile, Saul was still breathing out murderous threats against the Lord's disciples. He went to the high priest ² and asked him for letters to the synagogues in Damascus, so that if he found any there who belonged to the Way, whether men or women, he might take them as prisoners to Jerusalem. ³ As he neared Damascus on his journey, suddenly a light from heaven flashed around him. ⁴ He fell to the ground and heard a voice say to him, "Saul, Saul, why do you persecute me?" ⁵ "Who are you, Lord?" Saul asked. "I am Jesus, whom you are persecuting," he replied. ⁶ "Now get up and go into the city, and you will be told what you must do." ⁷ The men traveling with Saul stood there speechless; they heard the sound but did not see anyone. ⁸ Saul got up from the ground, but when he opened his eyes he could see nothing. So they led him by the hand into Damascus. ⁹ For three days he was blind, and did not eat or drink anything.

1 Meanwhile, Saul of Tarsus was still breathing out threats against the Lord's disciples. He saw no peaceful coexistence between Judaism and Christianity. With great intellect and passion, Saul was determined to destroy Christianity at home and abroad. He was looking for any believer he could lay his hands on.

Most believers had left Jerusalem. Aware of other believers in Damascus, He went to the high priest for permission to arrest them. The high priest was the head of Sanhedrin council. Damascus, the oldest city in the world, was the capital of Syria with a large Jewish population. It was a strategic commercial city located about 135 miles from Jerusalem.

2 Saul asked the high priest Caiaphas for letters of authority to the synagogues in Damascus, so that if he found any there who belonged to the Way, whether men or women, he might take them as prisoners to Jerusalem. Christianity was described as the Way in several places in Acts (e.g. Acts 19:9; 22:4; 24:14). It was called the Way because it was a way of life and Jesus is the way to eternal life (John 14:6). Saul's goal was to completely exterminate the Way.

3 With the permission, he headed north. As he neared Damascus on his journey, he was confronted by the risen Lord. Suddenly a light from heaven flashed around him. It was a supernatural light, brighter than the sun (Acts 26:13). It should be regarded as an expression of divine glory. A few seconds was enough to change the scoundrel Saul. The conversion of Saul is mentioned three times in Acts (Acts 9, 22, 26).

4 All his hatred, pride and zeal were ripped away in a moment. He was "slain in the Spirit." He fell to the ground and remained motionless. He heard a voice from the bright light asking him, "Saul, Saul, why do you persecute me?" As Saul was persecuting members of Christ's body, He was also persecuting Him, the head of the body. Touching a believer is touching Jesus. "The story of Saul's spiritual transformation ought to remind us never to write anyone off as being beyond the love of Christ."[1]

5 "Who are you, Lord?" Saul asked. "I am Jesus, whom you are persecuting," Jesus replied. Saul thought he was serving God, but in reality he had been persecuting Jesus. Without knowing it, Saul had violently persecuted the Messiah, the Son of David, the Son of God. The miraculous conversion is an example of the power of saving grace. The bloodthirsty hunter of God's saints now was now the hunted. A former blasphemer was turned in to a fervent believer (1 Timothy 1:13-17). His conversion occurred the moment he acknowledged Christ as Lord.

6 Jesus finally instructed him, "Now get up and go into the city, and you will be told what you must do." Jesus had a special work for Saul to do. In due time he would be told. From now on, he was a new man.

"The Hebrew of Hebrews would become the apostle of the Gentiles; the persecutor would become a preacher; and the legalistic Pharisee would become the great proclaimer of the grace of God."[2] God thoroughly humbled Saul and prepared him for the ministry of Ananias.

7 The men traveling with Saul stood there speechless. They saw the heavenly light, but they did not see the Lord. They heard the sound but did not understand what it meant. The men could not grasp the full significance of the encounter. They were less affected by the encounter. Only Saul understood the voice, and only he was blinded. The men were just there to support Saul.

8 Saul got up from the ground, but when he opened his eyes he could see nothing. So his companions led him by the hand into Damascus. The helpless persecutor was led into the city. He was blind, weak, and powerless. Saul became temporarily blind and never saw Christ, as some claim. He heard His voice, but did not see Him. Though his physical eyes were closed, his spiritual eyes were now open.

9 For three days he was blind, and did not eat or drink anything. Saul was crushed and humbled. Those three days were a period of meditation, fasting, and prayer for Saul. He was reevaluating his whole religious belief. He had prided himself on his religious background, education, and discipline in keeping the law. Saul later wrote, "Yes, everything else is worthless when compared with the priceless gain of knowing Christ Jesus my Lord. I have put aside all else, counting it worth less than nothing, in order that I can have Christ" (Philippians 3:8, TLB).

Ananias Sent to Saul

Verses 10-16: In Damascus there was a disciple named Ananias. The Lord called to him in a vision, "Ananias!" "Yes, Lord," he answered. [11] The Lord told him, "Go to the house of Judas on Straight Street and ask for a man from Tarsus named Saul, for he is praying. [12] In a vision he has seen a man named Ananias come and place his hands on him to restore his sight." [13] "Lord," Ananias answered, "I have heard many reports about this man and all the harm he has done to your holy people in Jerusalem. [14] And he has come here with authority from the chief priests to arrest all who call on your name."

¹⁵ But the Lord said to Ananias, "Go! This man is my chosen instrument to proclaim my name to the Gentiles and their kings and to the people of Israel. ¹⁶ I will show him how much he must suffer for my name."

10 In the city of Damascus, there was a disciple named Ananias. He was highly respected by the Jews living there (Acts 22:12). The Lord called to him in a vision, "Ananias!" "Yes, Lord," he answered. A vision is similar to a dream except that one is awake rather than sleeping. Joel prophesied that young men would see visions (Joel 2:28). God desires to communicate with us through dreams and visions. We must be willing to listen to Him.

11 In a vision, the Lord told Ananias, "Go to the house of Judas on Straight Street and ask for a man from Tarsus named Saul, for he is praying." The Lord told him where to find Saul of Tarsus. The Straight street still exists in Damascus today as the main east-west thoroughfare. This is the first of the five references in Acts to the place where Saul was born.

For three days, Saul was praying and fasting. He became a man of unceasing prayer. He was used to praying three times a day. One can guess that he prayed for forgiveness of his cruel persecution of the church.

12 The Lord told Ananias that in a vision Saul had seen a man named Ananias come and place his hands on him to restore his sight. We notice how the Lord worked on both ends. In two simultaneous visions, the Lord asked Ananias to go and pray for Saul, and He also showed Saul that Ananais was coming. Ananias was told that Saul would be expecting him.

13,14 "Lord," Ananias answered, "I have heard many reports about this man and all the harm he has done to your holy people in Jerusalem. And he has come here with authority from the chief priests to arrest all who call on your name." Ananias was understandably reluctant to go to Saul. The man had heard about the havoc Saul caused believers in Jerusalem and that he had come to Damascus for the same purpose—to arrest those who called on the Lord's name. He expressed his fears to the Lord. For him to go to Saul meant imprisonment and possibly death.

15 But the Lord said to Ananias, "Go! This man is my chosen instrument to proclaim my name to the Gentiles and their kings and to the people of Israel." This is a good summary of the life and ministry of Saul. Ananias should not worry about Saul's past life; Saul was now an instrument in the Lord's hand. It is an irony that the most anti-Gentile Jew would be chosen to take the gospel message to the Gentiles. Even Saul himself marveled to see himself as the recipient of such grace.

16 "I will show him how much he must suffer for my name." The Lord revealed to Ananias the task placed on Saul and the suffering he would experience. Instead of making the saints suffer, Saul would now do the suffering. For Saul to carry out his mission would not be an easy matter. It would entail much suffering (Colossians 1:24).

Ananias Ministers to Saul

Verses 17-19: Then Ananias went to the house and entered it. Placing his hands on Saul, he said, "Brother Saul, the Lord—Jesus, who appeared to you on the road as you were coming here—has sent me so that you may see again and be filled with the Holy Spirit." [18] Immediately, something like scales fell from Saul's eyes, and he could see again. He got up and was baptized, [19] and after taking some food, he regained his strength. Saul spent several days with the disciples in Damascus.

17 Ananias obeyed the Lord. He went to the house where he was instructed to go and entered it. Placing his hands on Saul, he said, "Brother Saul, the Lord—Jesus, who appeared to you on the road as you were coming here—has sent me so that you may see again and be filled with the Holy Spirit." Ananias totally accepted Saul by addressing him as "brother." What he said confirmed what Saul himself had received. For Saul, all things had become new. Although there is no record that Saul was filled with the Holy Spirit here, there is no reason to doubt this.

18 Immediately, something like scales fell from Saul's eyes, and he could see again. His healing was immediate. His blindness was gone. He got up and was baptized. Baptism must always follow conversion. One must publicly identify with Christ and His people by being baptized. "By that act he openly united with the very people he had hated and persecuted.

His hated enemies became his friends, while his former friends instantly became his enemies."[3]

19 Saul was weak because he had been fasting for three days. He broke the fast by taking some food and regained his strength. Saul spent an indefinite period of several days with Ananias and other disciples in Damascus. A mark of being born again is the desire to be in the company of fellow believers. This would help Saul learn the basics of Christianity from those who knew Christ before him.

NOTES

1. R. Kent Hughes, *Acts: The Church Afire* (Wheaton, IL: Crossway,1996), p. 127.
2. Warren W. Wiersbe, *Be Dynamic: Acts 1-12* (Colorado Springs, CO: David C. Cook, 1987), p. 133.
3. John MacArthur, *The MacArthur New Testament Commentary: Acts 1-12* (Chicago, IL: Moody Publishers, 1994), p. 274.

Chapter 20

THE WITNESS OF SAUL

Acts 9:20-31

Saul in Damascus

Verses 20-22: At once he began to preach in the synagogues that Jesus is the Son of God. ²¹ All those who heard him were astonished and asked, "Isn't he the man who raised havoc in Jerusalem among those who call on this name? And hasn't he come here to take them as prisoners to the chief priests?" ²² Yet Saul grew more and more powerful and baffled the Jews living in Damascus by proving that Jesus is the Messiah.

20 After spending a few days with fellow believers, he immediately began to preach in the synagogues that Jesus is the Son of God. This is the only place the title "Son of God" appears in Acts; Saul used it in his epistle at least fifteen times. Saul wasted no time in appearing in the synagogues proclaiming Christ. The gospel was too good to keep to himself; he must share it. "The most zealous defender of Judaism now became the most zealous evangelist for Christianity."[1] Saul is regarded as one of the most brilliant scholars who ever lived.

21 Time and time again Saul gave his testimony in the synagogues. The effect of his preaching must have been electrifying. All those who heard him were astonished and asked, "Isn't he the man who raised havoc in Jerusalem among those who call on this name? And hasn't he come here to take them as prisoners to the chief priests?" They remembered his mission in Damascus. They could not understand the sudden change in Saul.

22 Yet Saul grew more and more powerful and baffled the Jews living in Damascus by proving that Jesus is the Messiah. The more Saul understood who Jesus was, the more passionate he became in proclaiming Him. What caused the stir was that Saul was proving that Jesus was the Christ using his own Scriptures. Once the proof was made, people had to decide whether to believe or not.

A Plot to Kill Saul

Verses 23-25: After many days had gone by, there was a conspiracy among the Jews to kill him, ²⁴ but Saul learned of their plan. Day and night they kept close watch on the city gates in order to kill him. ²⁵ But his followers took him by night and lowered him in a basket through an opening in the wall.

23 After many days had gone by, there was a conspiracy among the Jews to kill him. Saul was too much for them and they wanted to do away with him. They could no longer tolerate his preaching of Jesus. They planned to silence him by assassination. A serious threat was placed on Saul's life. As Jerry Falwell used to say, "The man of God cannot die before his time." God had plans for Saul and would protect him.

24 Saul learned of their plan. An anonymous source informed him. Day and night his enemies kept close watch on the city gates in order to seize an opportunity to kill him. They probably did not want to kill him within the city and were waiting for the moment he would leave the city. They watched the gates 24/7 to make sure he did not escape. While the Jewish opponents were watching Saul, some loyal friends or followers were protecting him.

25 Some of the houses back then were built close to the city wall. Saul's followers took him by night and lowered him in a basket through an opening in the wall. This is the first of many narrow escapes Saul would experience. Both his entrance into Damascus and his departure were inglorious and memorable.

Saul left Damascus and stayed in Arabia for three years (Galatians 1:17, 18). He was there to spend time with God. "It is unclear whether Paul's three-year stay occurred between verses 22 and 23 or between verses 25 and 26."[2] Saul mentioned in the first chapter of Galatians that he went to Jerusalem three years after his conversion.

Saul in Jerusalem

Verses 26-28: When he came to Jerusalem, he tried to join the disciples, but they were all afraid of him, not believing that he really was a disciple. [27] But Barnabas took him and brought him to the apostles. He told them how Saul on his journey had seen the Lord and that the Lord had spoken to him, and how in Damascus he had preached fearlessly in the name of Jesus. [28] So Saul stayed with them and moved about freely in Jerusalem, speaking boldly in the name of the Lord.

26 Saul went to meet the brethren in Jerusalem, the headquarters of the NT church, and be part of them. But he was not received with enthusiasm. When he came to Jerusalem, he tried to join the disciples, but they were all still afraid of him, not believing that he really was a disciple. The saints in Jerusalem were suspicious of Saul. They were all afraid and did not believe what was said about his new experience.

27 But Barnabas took him and brought him to the apostles. He told them how Saul on his journey had seen the Lord and that the Lord had spoken to him, and how in Damascus he had preached fearlessly in the name of Jesus. We already met Barnabas (the "son of encouragement") in Acts 4:36,37. He lived up to his name. He was a hero of inclusiveness. Based on the recommendation of Barnabas, Saul was accepted by the apostles.

28 So Saul stayed with them for fifteen days (Galatians 1:18). He must have used part of that time to get to know Peter and the other apostles. He moved about freely in Jerusalem, speaking boldly in the name of the Lord. As he did in Damascus, Saul was again boldly proclaiming in the synagogues that Jesus is the Messiah. He was busy speaking and debating for the Lord.

A Plan to Kill Saul

Verses 29-31: He talked and debated with the Hellenistic Jews, but they tried to kill him. [30] When the believers learned of this, they took him down to Caesarea and sent him off to Tarsus. [31] Then the church throughout Judea, Galilee and Samaria enjoyed a time of peace and was strengthened. Living in the fear of the Lord and encouraged by the Holy Spirit, it increased in numbers.

29 Saul talked and debated with the Greek-speaking Jews, the Hellenists. He took the place of Stephen and stirred up controversy. They could not stand up against him. He found himself under threat from the same people that killed Stephen. They tried to kill him because of their intolerant attitude. They perceived that Saul was too dangerous to the survival of their religion—Judaism. "Wherever Paul went, his sermon either caused a revival or a riot."[3] Therefore, they sought ways to get rid of him.

30 When the believers learned of this, Saul was forced to escape for his life. They took him down to Caesarea and put him on a ship to Tarsus. Caesarea was on the coast and was located 57 miles northwest of Jerusalem. It was the home of Philip the evangelist. Saul eventually set sail and arrived at Tarsus, his birthplace. It was decided that the safest place for him would be his hometown of Tarsus, the capital city of Cilicia. One can expect Saul to begin to evangelizing his hometown right away.

31 Saul's departure from Jerusalem helped quiet conflicts with the Jews there. The church throughout Judea, Galilee and Samaria enjoyed a time of peace and was strengthened. That was partly due to the conversion of Saul, the most zealous persecutor of the church. The regions of Judea, Galilee, and Samaria formed the whole of Palestine. Living in the fear of the Lord and encouraged by the Holy Spirit, the church increased in numbers. With Saul in Tarsus, the focus of Acts now turns back to Peter.

NOTES

1. John MacArthur, *The MacArthur New Testament Commentary: Acts 1-12* (Chicago, IL: Moody Publishers, 1994), p. 275.
2. B. Bruce Barton et al., *Life Application Bible Commentary: Acts* (Carol Stream, IL: Tyndale House Publishers, 1999), p. 160.
3. Chuck Smith, *The Book of Acts* (Costa Mesa, CA: The Word for Today, 2013), p. 154.

Chapter 21

PETER'S MIGHTY WORKS

Acts 9:32-43

Peter's Ministry in Lydda

Verses 32-35: As Peter traveled about the country, he went to visit the Lord's people who lived in Lydda. [33] There he found a man named Aeneas, who was paralyzed and had been bedridden for eight years. [34] "Aeneas," Peter said to him, "Jesus Christ heals you. Get up and roll up your mat." Immediately Aeneas got up. [35] All those who lived in Lydda and Sharon saw him and turned to the Lord.

32 The focus now was on Peter. The apostles had concentrated too long in Jerusalem when the whole world was waiting for the message of the gospel. Peter, as the leader of the apostles, now embarked on an itinerant ministry intended to instruct and encourage believers. As Peter traveled about the country, he went to visit the Lord's people who lived in Lydda. That implies that a church had already been planted in Lydda. Lydda was called Lod in the OT (1 Chronicles 8:12) and was about 20 miles northwest of Jerusalem. Today it is the location of the Ben Gurion International Airport in Israel.

33 When Peter got to Lydda, he found a man named Aeneas, who was paralyzed and had been bedridden for eight years. His paralysis was beyond medical treatment at that time. The doctors had considered his case hopeless. The believers in Lydda might have faith but they lacked the spiritual gift of healing. Peter's being around was a blessing for the man.

34 Peter had the gift of healing, which should not be commercialized but used for the benefit of the body of Christ. "Aeneas," Peter said to him, "Jesus Christ heals you. Get up and roll up your mat." Immediately Aeneas got up. The healing was instantaneous and complete. It was not Peter that healed the man but Jesus Christ was the Healer. Peter did not promote himself but gave the credit to the Lord. He had been commissioned by the Lord to care for the sheep (John 21:15-17) and he was doing just that.

35 The miracle had a wonderful effect on people. All those who lived in Lydda and the neighboring town of Sharon saw him and turned to the Lord. The healing led to many conversions among the local residents. People were converted without hearing a sermon. The healing was enough for them to believe. This is why the church should not ignore the healing aspect of Christ's ministry today.

Peter's Ministry in Joppa

Verses 36-43: In Joppa there was a disciple named Tabitha (in Greek her name is Dorcas); she was always doing good and helping the poor. ³⁷ About that time she became sick and died, and her body was washed and placed in an upstairs room. ³⁸ Lydda was near Joppa; so when the disciples heard that Peter was in Lydda, they sent two men to him and urged him, "Please come at once!" ³⁹ Peter went with them, and when he arrived he was taken upstairs to the room. All the widows stood around him, crying and showing him the robes and other clothing that Dorcas had made while she was still with them. ⁴⁰ Peter sent them all out of the room; then he got down on his knees and prayed. Turning toward the dead woman, he said, "Tabitha, get up." She opened her eyes, and seeing Peter she sat up. ⁴¹ He took her by the hand and helped her to her feet. Then he called for the believers, especially the widows, and presented her to them alive. ⁴² This became known all over Joppa, and many people believed in the Lord. ⁴³ Peter stayed in Joppa for some time with a tanner named Simon.

36 In Joppa there was a disciple named Tabitha (in Greek her name is Dorcas). Joppa was 10 miles northwest of Lydda. Both Tabitha (in Hebrew/Aramaic) and Dorcas (in Greek) mean "gazelle." Dorcas lived up to that name. She was always doing good and helping the poor. She had the gift of helps. She fulfilled her calling as a disciple of Christ. She was a good NT example of a Proverbs 31 lady. It was tragic that she died when her usefulness to the body of Christ was most needed. She would be difficult to replace.

37 About that time she became sick and died. Her body was washed, but not anointed, and placed in an upstairs room to be further prepared for burial. They did not rush to bury her body as the custom required burying a corpse before sundown. Her death was a serious blow for the believers in Joppa. The believers had respect for Dorcas and strongly desired to see her restored to life.

38 Lydda was near Joppa; about 10 miles away. Joppa was a predominantly Jewish city. When the disciples heard that Peter was in Lydda, they sent a delegation of two men to him immediately. They urged him, "Please come at once!" Peter's presence was urgently needed. They were hoping and believing that Peter would raise Dorcas up since he had the power to heal. Jesus had raised up many people including the daughter of Jarius (Mark 5:40, 41); Peter was about to do the same.

39 Peter went with them, and when he arrived he was taken upstairs to the room where her body lay. All the widows stood around him, crying and showing him the robes and other clothing that Dorcas had made while she was still with them. There was no "government aid" back then and needy people (widows, orphans, foreigners, etc.) depended on caring people like Dorcas for their basic needs such as clothing.

40 As Peter had witnessed Jesus do when He raised Jairus' daughter, Peter sent the widows out of the room. He got down on his knees and prayed. Praying showed Peter's dependence on God. Turning toward the dead woman, he said, "Tabitha, get up." It was the power of God that raised Dorcas. She opened her eyes, and seeing Peter she sat up. One can only imagine how Peter felt as he performed this miracle—the greatest miracle God performed through him.

41 Peter took Dorcas by the hand and helped her to her feet. Peter did not accomplish this because of his inherent power. God had a reason He enabled him to raise a dead body here and nowhere else.

Peter called for the believers, especially the widows, and presented her to them—this back-from-the-dead saint. One can only imagine how the saints and widows felt when they saw Dorcas alive and well. They must have been filled with inexpressible joy.

42 Dorcas' return to life became known all over Joppa and the surrounding communities, and many people believed in the Lord. Just as with the healing of Aeneas, Dorcas' resurrection led many residents of Joppa to believe and trust Christ for their salvation. As Chuck Smith said, "Miracles of God lead to miracles of salvation."[1] The miracle was designed to authenticate the salvation message so that people who saw the sign might believe.

43 Peter stayed in Joppa for some time with a tanner (or leatherworker) named Simon. "Tanners were despised in first-century Jewish society, since they dealt with the skins of dead animals. Tanning was thus considered an unclean occupation, and Simon would have been shunned by the local synagogue."[2] God was gradually breaking down the walls separating people. The continual stream of converts in Joppa gave Peter plenty of work to do. Peter took time to ground the new believers in the Word of God.

NOTES

1. Chuck Smith, The Book of Acts (Costa Mesa, CA: The Word for Today, 2013), p. 158.
2. John MacArthur, The MacArthur New Testament Commentary: Acts 1-12 (Chicago, IL: Moody Publishers, 1994), p. 286.

Chapter 22

TWIN VISIONS

Acts 10:1-23

The Vision of Cornelius

Verses 1-8: At Caesarea there was a man named Cornelius, a centurion in what was known as the Italian Regiment. ² He and all his family were devout and God-fearing; he gave generously to those in need and prayed to God regularly. ³ One day at about three in the afternoon he had a vision. He distinctly saw an angel of God, who came to him and said, "Cornelius!" ⁴ Cornelius stared at him in fear. "What is it, Lord?" he asked. The angel answered, "Your prayers and gifts to the poor have come up as a memorial offering before God. ⁵ Now send men to Joppa to bring back a man named Simon who is called Peter. ⁶ He is staying with Simon the tanner, whose house is by the sea." ⁷ When the angel who spoke to him had gone, Cornelius called two of his servants and a devout soldier who was one of his attendants. ⁸ He told them everything that had happened and sent them to Joppa.

1 It was now time in God's providence to reconcile Jews and Gentiles in the body of Christ. The two individuals God would use to achieve this received visions from Him. At Caesarea there was a man named Cornelius, a centurion in what was known as the Italian Regiment. Caesarea was on the Mediterranean coast of Palestine. It was a seaport with large Gentile population. It was the Roman capital in Israel. "A Roman legion at full strength consisted of 6,000 men, and was divided into ten cohorts of 600 men each."[1] Due to frequent outbreaks of violence, Roman soldiers were stationed at Caesarea to keep peace in Israel.

2 He and all his family were devout and God-fearing. He had forsaken his pagan religion to worship the living Jehovah God. He gave generously to those in need and prayed to God regularly. But Cornelius lived outside the covenant people and had limited knowledge of God. God appreciated his genuineness in seeking Him and was making arrangements for him to know the Way.

3 One day at about three in the afternoon, the Jewish hour of evening prayer, he had a vision. When we have a vision, we can communicate with those in the spirit realm. He distinctly saw an angel of God, who came to him and addressed him by name. He would later describe this angel as "a man in shining clothes" (v. 30). The angel was sent by God to tell him what to do.

4 Cornelius stared at the angel in fear. He was terrified by the sight of the angel. We too will respond with fear if we suddenly see an angel in our room. "What is it, Lord?" he asked. The angel answered, "Your prayers and gifts to the poor have come up as a memorial offering before God." God keeps records of our good deeds. But God understood that good works could not save a soul. He arranged for Cornelius to hear the gospel of Jesus Christ through whom he could be saved.

5,6 The angel said, "Now send men to Joppa to bring back a man named Simon who is called Peter. He is staying with Simon the tanner, whose house is by the sea." He told Cornelius how to locate Peter in Joppa. Peter would tell him what to do. He would tell him about the Way of Christ. God could have allowed the angel to preach the gospel message to Cornelius, but He preferred to involve Peter in the important process of accepting Gentiles into His church. God uses human instruments to proclaim the gospel and do His work on earth.

7 When the angel who spoke to him had gone, Cornelius acted promptly in true military fashion. His promptness showed that he obeyed the angel's instructions. He understood how to give or receive orders. He called on two of his servants and a devout soldier who was one of his attendants. Two servants and a soldier, who shared his faith and could be trusted, were enough for the errand.

8 Cornelius told them everything that had happened and sent them to Joppa. He told them Peter's name, who he was staying with, and why Peter was needed. They were fully informed. Caesarea was about 30 miles from Joppa. They arrived by foot at 12 noon the following day. Cornelius had to wait for Peter for four days (v. 30). The next stage was how God would deal with Peter to meet Cornelius.

The Vision of Peter

Verses 9-16: About noon the following day as they were on their journey and approaching the city, Peter went up on the roof to pray. [10] He became hungry and wanted something to eat, and while the meal was being prepared, he fell into a trance. [11] He saw heaven opened and something like a large sheet being let down to earth by its four corners. [12] It contained all kinds of four-footed animals, as well as reptiles and birds. [13] Then a voice told him, "Get up, Peter. Kill and eat." [14] "Surely not, Lord!" Peter replied. "I have never eaten anything impure or unclean."[15] The voice spoke to him a second time, "Do not call anything impure that God has made clean." [16] This happened three times, and immediately the sheet was taken back to heaven.

9 The scene moved from Cornelius to Peter. Peter had to be prepared to receive the messengers from Cornelius. The two men were devout and prayed regularly to God. About noon the following day as they were on their journey and approaching the city, Peter went up on the roof of the house he was staying at to pray. The roof of the house served as a patio and a good place to pray. Peter wanted to spend some time in fellowship with God, but God had a different plan.

10 It was time for lunch and Peter became hungry and wanted something to eat. While the meal was being prepared downstairs in Simon the tanner's house, he suddenly fell into a trance. God used that waiting time to get Peter's attention. The trance was conditioned by his immediate circumstances. "A trance is different from a vision. In a 'trance' the bodily senses are active and awake."[2] Although this verse calls Peter's experience a trance, verse 17 calls it a vision.

11 In the trance, he saw heaven open up and something like a large sheet being let down to earth from heaven by its four corners. When heaven opens, we see heavenly stuff. When Stephen saw heaven open earlier in Acts, He saw the Son of Man standing at the right hand of God (Acts 7:56). When Peter saw heaven open, he saw a large sheet being let down.

12 The sheet contained all kinds of four-footed animals, as well as reptiles and birds—the three categories of living creatures mentioned in the OT (Genesis 6:20). It was a mixture of clean and unclean creatures designed to disgust an orthodox Jew like Peter. As Peter was thinking about food, God showed him all kinds of animals. He used them as a basis of the instructions for Peter.

13 Then a voice told Peter, "Get up, Peter. Kill and eat." God commanded Peter to kill the creatures and begin to eat them as an act of devotion and service to Him. But the suggestion horrified him. His confusion was understandable. He was not hungry enough for that. God used this incident to teach Peter an important spiritual lesson. He would soon realize that he should not regard any group of people common or unclean. Peter was being prepared to receive Cornelius' messengers.

14 "Surely not, Lord!" Peter replied. "I have never eaten anything impure or unclean." As an orthodox Jew, Peter was following the OT instructions restricting Israelites from eating unclean creatures (Leviticus 11; Deuteronomy 14). Those dietary restrictions separated Israel from other nations. However, the day for those restrictions was over.

15 The voice spoke to Peter a second time, "Do not call anything impure that God has made clean." He was asked not to label impure what God had made clean. His worldview was under threat. He would need to change his attitude as those OT restrictions were no longer binding. Jesus had declared all foods to be clean (Mark 7:15, 16). "It has been suggested that Acts 10 is as much about the conversion of Peter (from racial prejudice) as it is about the conversion of Cornelius."[3]

16 This happened three times, and immediately the sheet was taken back to heaven. Although it was repeated three times, Peter could not make any sense out of it. He continued to exhibit piety beyond the will of God. However, the threefold repetition of the statement "Do not call anything impure that God has made clean" would ring hard in Peter's mind.

Peter Meets the Messengers

Verses 17-23: While Peter was wondering about the meaning of the vision, the men sent by Cornelius found out where Simon's house was and stopped at the gate. ¹⁸ They called out, asking if Simon who was known as Peter was staying there. ¹⁹ While Peter was still thinking about the vision, the Spirit said to him, "Simon, three men are looking for you. ²⁰ So get up and go downstairs. Do not hesitate to go with them, for I have sent them." ²¹ Peter went down and said to the men, "I'm the one you're looking for. Why have you come?" ²² The men replied, "We have come from Cornelius the centurion. He is a righteous and God-fearing man, who is respected by all the Jewish people. A holy angel told him to ask you to come to his house so that he could hear what you have to say." ²³ Then Peter invited the men into the house to be his guests. The next day Peter started out with them, and some of the believers from Joppa went along.

17 Peter was perplexed about the vision. Some have suggested the meaning of the vision: the unclean animals in the sheet represented the Gentiles, while the clean animals represented the Jews. While Peter was wondering about the meaning of the vision, the men sent by Cornelius found out where Simon's house was and stopped at the gate. They possibly did not have trouble locating the house.

18 They knocked on the door and called out, asking if Simon who was known as Peter was staying there. God's timing is perfect. Cornelius' messengers arrived at the door of Simon the tanner's house when Peter was still meditating on the vision. God did not let Peter speculate for too long. These men would help Peter understand the meaning of the vision.

19,20 While Peter was still thinking about the vision, the Spirit said to him, "Simon, three men are looking for you. So get up and go downstairs. Do not hesitate to go with them, for I have sent them." The three men (two servants and a soldier) sent by Cornelius were waiting for Peter downstairs. God sovereignly arranged for Peter to meet the three men. The Spirit convinced Peter that the vision and the men were connected and that he should do what they requested without hesitation.

21 Although Peter resisted the Spirit's voice during the vision, he obeyed the Spirit. He went down and met the men at the gate that separated the

house from the street. He said to the men, "I'm the one you're looking for. Why have you come?" He received the messengers and made himself known to the men. He wanted to know the nature of their mission.

22 The men explained the purpose of their visit. They said, "We have come from Cornelius the centurion. He is a righteous and God-fearing man, who is respected by all the Jewish people. A holy angel told him to ask you to come to his house so that he could hear what you have to say." The men told Peter about their master—a righteous man that feared God. They told him that an angel appeared to Cornelius and asked him to send for Peter. As Steven Ger put it, "Cornelius' men informed Peter of five fast facts about Cornelius: his position as a centurion, his characteristic righteousness, his status as a God-fearer, his excellent reputation among the Jewish people, and that he had been directed by an angel to meet with Peter in Caesarea."[4]

23 Then Peter invited the men into the house to be his guests. It was too late for them to go back to Caesarea that day. Though he was a guest himself, Peter offered them hospitality for the night. His bold step of lodging the three Gentile men was an indication that the barriers between Jews and Gentiles were coming down. The next day Peter started out with them, and some of the believers from Joppa went along. It was wise on Peter's part to allow six brothers (Acts 11:12) from Joppa to accompany him to Caesarea and be witnesses. The ten men walked towards Caesarea.

NOTES

1. John MacArthur, *The MacArthur New Testament Commentary: Acts 1-12* (Chicago, IL: Moody Publishers, 1994), p. 293.
2. H. Leo Boles, *Acts* (Nashville, TN: Gospel Advocate Co., 1989), p. 163.
3. Derek W. H. Thomas, *Acts: Reformed Expository Commentary* (Phillipsburg, NJ: P&R Publishing Co., 2011), p. 287.
4. Steven Ger, *The Book of Acts: Witnesses to the World* (Chattanooga, TN: AMG Publishers, 2004), p. 156.

Chapter 23

GENTILE SALVATION

Acts 10:24-48

Peter Meets Cornelius

Verses 24-33: The following day he arrived in Caesarea. Cornelius was expecting them and had called together his relatives and close friends. 25 As Peter entered the house, Cornelius met him and fell at his feet in reverence. 26 But Peter made him get up. "Stand up," he said, "I am only a man myself." 27 While talking with him, Peter went inside and found a large gathering of people. 28 He said to them: "You are well aware that it is against our law for a Jew to associate with or visit a Gentile. But God has shown me that I should not call anyone impure or unclean. 29 So when I was sent for, I came without raising any objection. May I ask why you sent for me?" 30 Cornelius answered: "Three days ago I was in my house praying at this hour, at three in the afternoon. Suddenly a man in shining clothes stood before me 31 and said, 'Cornelius, God has heard your prayer and remembered your gifts to the poor. 32 Send to Joppa for Simon who is called Peter. He is a guest in the home of Simon the tanner, who lives by the sea.' 33 So I sent for you immediately, and it was good of you to come. Now we are all here in the presence of God to listen to everything the Lord has commanded you to tell us."

24 The following day Peter with nine other men arrived in Caesarea. They probably went on foot and took nine or ten hours. Cornelius was expecting them. He was busy making preparations. He had called together his relatives and close friends. He wanted them to hear what the

mysterious Simon Peter had to say. They came with prepared hearts and minds.

25 As Peter entered the house, Cornelius met him and fell at his feet in reverence. Cornelius probably did this out of gratitude for Peter's coming from Joppa to his house and for being in the presence of a messenger of God. He appreciated Peter's coming. Cornelius humbly knelt down before Peter and made obeisance. That way of reverencing Peter bordered on worship and was inappropriate and unbecoming to him.

26 How easy would it have been easy for Peter to accept worship and take advantage of the situation to promote himself. But Peter was embarrassed. He made Cornelius get up. "Stand up," he said, "I am only a man myself." "Some people today worship the stars—movie stars, rock stars, and sports stars."[1] No human being deserves worship. Only God should be worshipped.

27 While talking with him, Peter went inside and found a large gathering of people. Cornelius desperately wanted the truth for himself, his relatives, and his friends. Saving just one person would not send any wave to the church in Jerusalem. Saving a group of Gentiles would let the Jerusalem church know that the Gentiles were being included in the church.

28,29 Peter said to them: "You are well aware that it is against our law for a Jew to associate with or visit a Gentile. But God has shown me that I should not call anyone impure or unclean. So when I was sent for, I came without raising any objection. May I ask why you sent for me?" Every Gentile knew how the Jews avoided having social contact with the Gentiles. Ordinarily a Jew would not lodge a Gentile into his house. But Peter was saying that there was no longer a basis for separating Jews and Gentiles. Christianity is universal and inclusive; it transcends all cultures. There are no second-class people in the church of God (Colossians 3:11).

30 Cornelius simply repeated his experience with the angel that appeared to him. He said: "Three days ago I was in my house praying at this hour, at three in the afternoon. Suddenly a man in shining clothes stood before me." God can hear our prayer anywhere. Cornelius was in his house, not at the temple or synagogue, and God heard him. The "man in shinning clothes" was an angel of God, sent to deliver a message to Cornelius.

31,32 The angel said, "Cornelius, God has heard your prayer and remembered your gifts to the poor. Send to Joppa for Simon who is called Peter. He is a guest in the home of Simon the tanner, who lives by the sea." Cornelius had a good testimony in heaven. He was a man who was devoted to prayer and feared God. God remembered his good deeds to the poor. The angel asked Cornelius to summon Simon Peter and told him where Peter could be found.

33 "So I sent for you immediately, and it was good of you to come. Now we are all here in the presence of God to listen to everything the Lord has commanded you to tell us." Without delay Cornelius sent messengers to go and invite Peter. He was grateful that Peter honored his invitation and came so quickly. He was sure that God was about to talk to them through Peter. He now turned over the meeting to Peter.

Peter's Sermon

Verses 34-43: Then Peter began to speak: "I now realize how true it is that God does not show favoritism [35] *but accepts from every nation the one who fears him and does what is right.* [36] *You know the message God sent to the people of Israel, announcing the good news of peace through Jesus Christ, who is Lord of all.* [37] *You know what has happened throughout the province of Judea, beginning in Galilee after the baptism that John preached—* [38] *how God anointed Jesus of Nazareth with the Holy Spirit and power, and how he went around doing good and healing all who were under the power of the devil, because God was with him.* [39] *"We are witnesses of everything he did in the country of the Jews and in Jerusalem. They killed him by hanging him on a cross,* [40] *but God raised him from the dead on the third day and caused him to be seen.* [41] *He was not seen by all the people, but by witnesses whom God had already chosen—by us who ate and drank with him after he rose from the dead.* [42] *He commanded us to preach to the people and to testify that he is the one whom God appointed as judge of the living and the dead.* [43] *All the prophets testify about him that everyone who believes in him receives forgiveness of sins through his name."*

34,35 Then Peter began to speak: "I now realize how true it is that God does not show favoritism but accepts from every nation the one who fears him and does what is right." Based on the vision Peter saw he became convinced that God shows no partiality and is no respecter of persons. He accepts people into His kingdom irrespective of their gender, status, race, nationality, and position. He does not base His choice on external differences. Peter just realized that a God-fearing Gentile was just as good in the sight of God as a God-fearing Jew. As far as sin and salvation are concerned, there is no difference. "The barrier between Jew and Gentile had been removed in Christ. God is no 'respecter of persons,' but he is a respecter of character."[2]

36 "You know the message God sent to the people of Israel, announcing the good news of peace through Jesus Christ, who is Lord of all." The message of salvation was first offered to the Jews (Romans 1:16). Jesus came to preach the message of peace. He is the Lord and Creator of the universe; every person is accountable to Him. Peter assumed that his audience was familiar with the story of Jesus. Since Caesarea was in Palestine, it was likely that all Palestine had heard about Jesus.

37 The Word of God came first to the Jews. "You know what has happened throughout the province of Judea, beginning in Galilee after the baptism that John preached." Peter's audience also knew what happened in Judea. Starting from the baptism of John, Peter highlighted the work of Jesus. After John the Baptist preached, the ministry of Jesus started. His life was firmly based in history. He was going about doing good, preaching, teaching, and healing the sick.

38 "How God anointed Jesus of Nazareth with the Holy Spirit and power, and how He went around doing good and healing all who were under the power of the devil, because God was with Him." Here we notice that the three Persons within the Godhead were working cooperatively for the redemption of man. God set His Son apart. Jesus was equipped and empowered by the Holy Spirit. He used His anointing to do good, heal the sick, and deliver the oppressed.

39,40 "We are witnesses of everything he did in the country of the Jews and in Jerusalem. They killed him by hanging him on a cross, but God raised him from the dead on the third day and caused him to be seen." The apostles were living witnesses to the ministry of Jesus. The religious leaders murdered Him by crucifixion. They were responsible for His killing. But God vindicated His Son by raising Him from the dead. The resurrection is the essence of our faith. Without it, our faith is worthless (1 Corinthians 15:17).

41 "He was not seen by all the people, but by witnesses whom God had already chosen—by us who ate and drank with him after he rose from the dead." The risen Christ did not appear to everyone but only to a select group of believers including Peter. The resurrection appearances were numerous enough to convince anyone with an open mind. Peter alluded to the fact that the risen Jesus actually ate and drank with them.

42 Jesus commanded the apostles to preach His message to the people (Matthew 28:19). They were also to testify that He is the one whom God appointed as judge of the living and the dead. The Father loved the Son and committed everything into His hand including judgment (John 3:35; 5:22). "Christ is the only judge appointed by God to judge every person who has ever lived—past, present and future."[3]

43 All the prophets testified about Jesus (e.g. Isaiah 11:2; 42:1; Ezekiel 36:25,26). He was the fulfillment of the OT Messianic promises. What Jesus did was spoken by these prophets some centuries earlier. All the prophets pointed to Jesus and agreed that salvation is found only in Him.

Finally, Peter now presented the good news: "Everyone who believes in him receives forgiveness of sins through his name." Jesus was the long-awaited Savior who came to forgive sins. To every person there is a remedy for sin. Forgiveness comes by faith in Jesus alone. Those who do not accept Christ will remain in their sins and face Jesus as judge later. Peter's audience must decide for Jesus.

Cornelius' Salvation

Verses 44-48: While Peter was still speaking these words, the Holy Spirit came on all who heard the message. ⁴⁵ The circumcised believers who had come with Peter were astonished that the gift of the Holy Spirit had been poured out even on Gentiles. ⁴⁶ For they heard them speaking in tongues and *praising God. Then Peter said, *[47]* "Surely no one can stand in the way of their being baptized with water. They have received the Holy Spirit just as we have." *[48]* So he ordered that they be baptized in the name of Jesus Christ. Then they asked Peter to stay with them for a few days.*

44 While Peter was still speaking these words, the Holy Spirit came on all who heard the message. The Holy Spirit sovereignly interrupted Peter's message. It was as if the Holy Spirit was saying to Peter, "They have heard enough." There was no need for a conclusion or an invitation to receive Christ. The audience received the baptism of the Holy Spirit immediately. This event has been called the "Gentile Pentecost."

45 The six circumcised (Jews) believers who had come with Peter were astonished that the gift of the Holy Spirit had been poured out even on Gentiles. The Holy Spirit was given to them as an undeniable evidence that the Gentiles were truly saved and that they were now on a level equal to Jewish believers. They learned first hand that the gospel was inclusive.

46,47 For they heard them speaking in tongues and praising God. Speaking in tongues was a sure evidence or a visible proof that they had received the Holy Spirit. This sign gift was necessary. Then Peter said, "Surely no one can stand in the way of their being baptized with water. They have received the Holy Spirit just as we have." Peter could not refuse the lesser sign to these Gentiles when God had already given them the greater sign. Water baptism always follows salvation. It is a symbolic way of identifying with Christ in His death, burial, and resurrection. This is the only place in Acts where the Spirit comes before baptism in water.

48 So Peter ordered that they be baptized in the name of Jesus Christ. Baptism was the first public act of obedience to the Lord. The baptism of Cornelius, his household, and his friends was probably done by Peter and the six brothers that came with Peter.

Then the new believers at Caesarea asked Peter to stay with them for a few days. They wanted to learn more from Peter and enjoy his fellowship. While the gift of the Spirit was present, they wanted to have human teachers too.

NOTES

1. Chuck Smith, *The Book of Acts* (Costa Mesa, CA: The Word for Today, 2013), p. 168.
2. H. Leo Boles, *Acts* (Nashville, TN: Gospel Advocate Co., 1989), p. 171.
3. Derek Carlsen, *Faith & Courage: Commentary on Acts* (Arlington Heights, IL: Christian Liberty Press, 2000), p. 270.

Chapter 24

PETER'S DEFENSE

Acts 11:1-18

Peter is Criticized

Verses 1-3: The apostles and the believers throughout Judea heard that the Gentiles also had received the word of God. ² So when Peter went up to Jerusalem, the circumcised believers criticized him ³ and said, "You went into the house of uncircumcised men and ate with them."

1 The apostles and the believers throughout Judea heard that the Gentiles had also received the Word of God and had been admitted into the body of Christ. News travels fast, far and wide in a small country like Palestine. The news about the Gentile conversion reached Jerusalem and Judea before Peter got there since he stayed in Caesarea for a while.

2,3 When Peter finally went up to Jerusalem, the circumcised believers criticized him and said, "You went into the house of uncircumcised men and ate with them." He was confronted by the strong legalistic, circumcision party in the church. The social implication of fellowshipping with the Gentiles was disturbing to them. They believed that there should be no interaction between the circumcised and uncircumcised. In their eyes, for Gentiles to become Christians, they must be circumcised and become Jewish proselytes. They would not expect Peter to visit Gentile homes and eat with them. Peter had ceremonially defiled himself and broken the taboo.

Peter Explains the Vision

Verses 4-10: Starting from the beginning, Peter told them the whole story:
⁵ "I was in the city of Joppa praying, and in a trance I saw a vision. I saw
something like a large sheet being let down from heaven by its four corners,
and it came down to where I was. ⁶ I looked into it and saw four-footed
animals of the earth, wild beasts, reptiles and birds. ⁷ Then I heard a voice
telling me, 'Get up, Peter. Kill and eat.' ⁸ "I replied, 'Surely not, Lord!
Nothing impure or unclean has ever entered my mouth.' ⁹ "The voice spoke
from heaven a second time, 'Do not call anything impure that God has made
clean.' ¹⁰ This happened three times, and then it was all pulled up to heaven
again.

4 The accusers criticized Peter before they gathered their information.
Peter did not argue with the accusers about their prejudice. He explained
to them the events that led to the conversion of the Gentiles. Starting
from the beginning, Peter patiently told them the whole story: He
defended what he had done. Luke now rehearses the whole story again.

5 "I was in the city of Joppa praying, and in a trance I saw a vision. I
saw something like a large sheet being let down from heaven by its four
corners, and it came down to where I was." Peter shared the vision he
had, hoping that they would understand. He retold the vision at Joppa
and its God-given interpretation. Change and expansion come through
men and women who dream or have a vision. Peter emphasized God's
initiative and blamed the Holy Spirit for all that took place.

6 It was while Peter was praying that he saw the vision. "I looked into it
and saw four-footed animals of the earth, wild beasts, reptiles and birds."
The list of creatures has expanded to include "wild breasts." The sheet
descending from heaven was filled with creatures that were ceremonially
unclean. This reminds one of the dietary laws of Leviticus 11, which
Peter's accusers knew very well.

7-9 Then Peter heard a voice telling him, "Get up, Peter. Kill and eat."
This command was not obeyed by Peter. God was working on Peter
whose views needed challenging at the fundamental level.

Peter replied, "Surely not, Lord! Nothing impure or unclean has ever entered my mouth." He refused to kill and eat these animals because they were ceremonially unclean.

The voice spoke from heaven a second time, "Do not call anything impure that God has made clean." A voice from heaven instructed Peter not to call impure what God has made clean.

10 This happened three times, and then it was all pulled up to heaven again. Even the dullest scholar could hardly miss the point when a lesson was repeated three times by the teacher. Some commentators claim that the same instructions were repeated three times to confirm that it was from the Lord, not from the demonic world.

Peter's Call to Caesarea

Verses 11-14: "Right then three men who had been sent to me from Caesarea stopped at the house where I was staying. [12] The Spirit told me to have no hesitation about going with them. These six brothers also went with me, and we entered the man's house. [13] He told us how he had seen an angel appear in his house and say, 'Send to Joppa for Simon who is called Peter. [14] He will bring you a message through which you and all your household will be saved.'

11 "Right then three men who had been sent to me from Caesarea stopped at the house where I was staying." While Peter was still meditating on the vision, the three men Cornelius had sent arrived. Peter understood that God was behind all this and cooperated. God knew the next step Peter and the church needed to take to make the church inclusive.

12 The Spirit told Peter to have no hesitation about going with them. Six brothers from the Joppa church also went with Peter, and they entered the man's house at Caesarea. The Holy Spirit was in business. Peter was led by the Spirit and as the Spirit led, all was done in proper order. He was accompanied by six brethren, twice the number demanded by the Law. Peter brought these brethren with him to Jerusalem as witnesses.

13,14 Peter now narrated Cornelius' side of the story. Cornelius told Peter and the six brothers how he had seen an angel appear in his house and say, "Send to Joppa for Simon who is called Peter. He will bring you a message through which you and all your household will be saved." This verse shows that Cornelius and his household were not saved until Peter's arrival. It was Peter who preached the message of salvation.

Cornelius Received the Spirit

Verses 15-18: "As I began to speak, the Holy Spirit came on them as he had come on us at the beginning. ¹⁶ Then I remembered what the Lord had said: 'John baptized with water, but you will be baptized with the Holy Spirit.' ¹⁷ So if God gave them the same gift he gave us who believed in the Lord Jesus Christ, who was I to think that I could stand in God's way?" ¹⁸ When they heard this, they had no further objections and praised God, saying, "So then, even to Gentiles God has granted repentance that leads to life."

15 "As I began to speak, the Holy Spirit came on them as he had come on us at the beginning"—at Pentecost. God had added Gentiles to the body of Christ. As John Phillips said, "Cornelius and the Gentiles had been accepted by God as equal heirs of the grace of God, first-class citizens in the kingdom, fellow members of the Body of Christ."[1]

16 Then Peter remembered what the Lord had said: "John baptized with water, but you will be baptized with the Holy Spirit" (Acts 1:5). We are all given the Holy Spirit when we are saved. By one Spirit, we have all been baptized into one body (1 Corinthians 12:13). Water baptism is different from the baptism in the Holy Spirit (Matthew 3:11). "I do not concur with those who say the gifts and the empowering of the Holy Spirit disappeared at the end of the apostolic age."[2]

17 "So if God gave them the same gift he gave us who believed in the Lord Jesus Christ, who was I to think that I could stand in God's way?" No one can withstand God or stand in His way. God has the right to do what He wants, with whom He wants, whenever He wants. Who dares ask God, "What are you doing?" (Job 9:12). Whoever contends with God is inviting trouble and hardship.

18 When they heard Peter's defense, they had no further objections. His accusers held their peace. They could not argue with the Holy Spirit and the six witnesses. The critics praised God, saying, "So then, even to Gentiles God has granted repentance that leads to life." What a difference it makes when we see others with loving, inclusive attitudes.

NOTES

1. John Phillips, *Exploring Acts* (Grand Rapids, MI: Kregel Publications, 1986), p. 215.
2. Chuck Smith, *The Book of Acts* (Costa Mesa, CA: The Word for Today, 2013), p. 183.

Chapter 25

THE CHURCH AT ANTIOCH

Acts 11:19-30

The Genesis

Verses 19-21: Now those who had been scattered by the persecution that broke out when Stephen was killed traveled as far as Phoenicia, Cyprus and Antioch, spreading the word only among Jews. ²⁰ Some of them, however, men from Cyprus and Cyrene, went to Antioch and began to speak to Greeks also, telling them the good news about the Lord Jesus. ²¹ The Lord's hand was with them, and a great number of people believed and turned to the Lord.

19 Now those who had been scattered by the persecution that broke out when Stephen was killed preached the Word wherever they went (Acts 8:4). Some of them traveled as far as Phoenicia, Cyprus and Antioch, spreading the Word only among Jews. Others went to other places such as Samaria, Caesarea, Damascus, Lydda, Joppa, and Sharon. These were the places the believers were scattered due to the persecuton in Jerusalem. They still assumed that the gospel was exclusively for the Jews.

20 Some of them, however, men from Cyprus and Cyrene, went to Antioch in Syria. "Cyprus was an island off the Mediterranean coast from Antioch, and Cyrene was a city in northern Africa."[1] Antioch was the third largest city at that time, surpassed in population only by Rome and Alexandria. It had a predominantly Gentile population with a significant minority of Jews.

At Antioch, the men began to speak to Greeks also, telling them the good news about the Lord Jesus. Antioch was about 300 miles north of

Jerusalem. The Greek-speaking Jews from Cyprus and Cyrene found it easier to reach the Gentiles for Christ.

21 The Lord's hand was with them because they were doing what pleased Him. The hand of the Lord referred to His power expressed in blessing the work and making His power visible and tangible. The Lord was pleased because Gentiles were being reached with the gospel. A great number of people believed and turned to the Lord. The gospel message was like bread to the hungry. The people were hungry for the truth.

Antioch's Growth

Verses 22-26: News of this reached the church in Jerusalem, and they sent Barnabas to Antioch. ²³ When he arrived and saw what the grace of God had done, he was glad and encouraged them all to remain true to the Lord with all their hearts. ²⁴ He was a good man, full of the Holy Spirit and faith, and a great number of people were brought to the Lord. ²⁵ Then Barnabas went to Tarsus to look for Saul, ²⁶ and when he found him, he brought him to Antioch. So for a whole year Barnabas and Saul met with the church and taught great numbers of people. The disciples were called Christians first at Antioch.

22 The news of what was going on at Antioch reached the church in Jerusalem. They sent Barnabas to Antioch to investigate. Barnabas was a Greek-speaking Jew, raised on the island of Cyprus. We recall that Barnabas sold his land and brought the money to the church at Jerusalem (Acts 4:37). It was Barnabas who introduced Saul to the apostles (Acts 9:27). He was just the right man for the job. Without hesitation, he accepted the new work.

23 When Barnabas arrived and saw the outward observable expressions of what the grace of God had done, he was glad. He rejoiced at what the Lord was doing at Antioch. As the Son of Encouragement, Barnabas encouraged them all to remain true to the Lord with all their hearts. The way to remain true to the Lord is to abide in the Lord and continue in His Word. Barnabas' message focused on the complete commitment of believers.

24 Barnabas was a good man, full of the Holy Spirit and faith. His qualities are comparable to those of Stephen (Acts 6:5). He was a Christlike person in character and conduct. He was the kind of a believer we would all like to emulate. Before Barnabas came, a great number had been added. A large crowds of people responded favorably and were brought to the Lord through him.

25 The harvest was too much for one person to handle. Before long Barnabas realized he needed an assistant to effectively pastor the church in Antioch. So Barnabas went to Tarsus to look for Saul, somebody he could trust. Saul was a man of great zeal for the Lord and sound spiritual anointing. Finding Saul in his hometown was not easy since it had been a while he left Jerusalem for Tarsus.

26 When Barnabas found Saul, he brought him to Antioch. So for a whole year Barnabas and Saul met with the church and taught great numbers of people. The two men formed an awesome ministry team. They taught, not preached, the Word. When people give their lives to Christ, they need teaching to grow.

The disciples were called Christians first at Antioch. The name "Christians" means followers of Christ or Christ-like persons and is appropriate for believers in Christ. Although it was a derogatory name coined by unbelievers in Antioch, believers liked it and got stuck with it.

Antioch's Generosity

Verses 27-30: During this time some prophets came down from Jerusalem to Antioch. ²⁸ One of them, named Agabus, stood up and through the Spirit predicted that a severe famine would spread over the entire Roman world. (This happened during the reign of Claudius.) ²⁹ The disciples, as each one was able, decided to provide help for the brothers and sisters living in Judea. ³⁰ This they did, sending their gift to the elders by Barnabas and Saul.

27 During this time some prophets came down from Jerusalem to Antioch. The church at Jerusalem could not ignore what was going on in the church at Antioch. They sent some prophets. Prophets were Christ's gift to His church (Ephesians 4:11). These NT prophets, like their OT counterparts, were capable of receiving direct revelation from God and predicting the future. Paul ranked prophets second only to the apostles (1 Corinthians 12:28) in the five different offices in the church. These were not just preachers, as some claim. The gift of prophecy has not ceased to operate in the church.

28 It seems that prophets in the early church were traveling from place to place. One of them, named Agabus, stood up and through the Spirit predicted that a severe famine would spread over the entire Roman world. A test of a genuine prophet is that his prophecy must come to pass. In this case of Agabus, his prediction came to pass during the time of the Emperor Claudius, who ruled from A.D. 41-54.

29 The disciples, as each one was able, decided to provide help for the brothers and sisters living in Judea when the famine hit. Believers in Antioch determined to help their fellow believers in Judea who were severely affected by the famine. That is real Christianity in action. "If one member suffers, all suffer together" (1 Corinthians 12:26, RSV). Everybody gave according to their means. Their generosity was an expression of love by the Gentile believers. Contrary to our expectation, money flowed from the mission field to the homeland, not the other way around.

30 This they did, sending their gift to the elders in Judea through Barnabas and Saul. The church in Antioch had confidence in these two leaders. They were to take the "relief offering" to the financially suffering church in Jerusalem. They would travel many miles together and minister to people along the way. They complemented each other. We recall that Barnabas was sent to Antioch by the church in Jerusalem. For Paul, this was his second trip to Jerusalem since his conversion. The first time he was not well received. Barnabas had to introduce him to the apostles. We can be sure that he got a warm reception this time.

NOTES

1. B. Bruce Barton et al., *Life Application Bible Commentary: Acts* (Carol Stream, IL: Tyndale House Publishers, 1999), p. 194.

Chapter 26

PETER'S GREAT ESCAPE

Acts 12:1-17

Herod Persecutes the Church

Verses 1-4: It was about this time that King Herod arrested some who belonged to the church, intending to persecute them. ² He had James, the brother of John, put to death with the sword. ³ When he saw that this met with approval among the Jews, he proceeded to seize Peter also. This happened during the Festival of Unleavened Bread. ⁴ After arresting him, he put him in prison, handing him over to be guarded by four squads of four soldiers each. Herod intended to bring him out for public trial after the Passover.

1 It was about this time that King Herod arrested some who belonged to the church, intending to persecute them. The Herod mentioned here was Herod Agrippa I. He reigned over Judea from A.D. 37 to A.D. 44. He was a grandson of Herod the Great, who reigned from 37 B.C. to 4 B.C. and sought to kill infant Jesus (Matthew 2:16). Herod Agrippa sought to win favor with the Jewish authorities by persecuting the church.

2 King Herod had apostle James, the brother of John, put him to death with the sword. James and John were sons of Zebedee, a fisherman in Galilee. James was the first apostle to die as a martyr, while his brother John was the last apostle to die. They both drank the same cup as their Master and shared in the baptism of suffering (Matthew 20:23). They both were called the "the sons of thunder" by Jesus. James was the only apostle whose death is recorded in the NT.

3 When King Herod saw that this met with approval among the Jews, he proceeded to seize Peter also. Peter was the acknowledged leader of the church and his execution would be a severe blow to the church. This happened during the Festival of Unleavened Bread, which usually lasted for a week. Since these were holy days, Herod's plan was to have Peter imprisoned during the festival and then execute him after it was over. Peter had been imprisoned twice before (Acts 4:3; 5:18).

4 After arresting him, King Herod put him in prison, handing him over to be guarded by four squads of four soldiers each. Herod intended to bring him out for public trial after the Passover. Peter was kept in the maximum security section of Herod's prison and watched by sixteen soldiers, in shifts of four. All this was done for one person who had broken no law. The human possibility of escape was nil. "Like so many before him, Agrippa was to learn the folly of fighting God...Three reasons for not fighting God stand out in Acts 12: God's power cannot be contested, His punishment cannot be avoided, and His purposes cannot be frustrated."[1]

Peter Imprisoned and Delivered

Verses 5-11: So Peter was kept in prison, but the church was earnestly praying to God for him. ⁶ The night before Herod was to bring him to trial, Peter was sleeping between two soldiers, bound with two chains, and sentries stood guard at the entrance. ⁷ Suddenly an angel of the Lord appeared and a light shone in the cell. He struck Peter on the side and woke him up. "Quick, get up!" he said, and the chains fell off Peter's wrists. ⁸ Then the angel said to him, "Put on your clothes and sandals." And Peter did so. "Wrap your cloak around you and follow me," the angel told him. ⁹ Peter followed him out of the prison, but he had no idea that what the angel was doing was really happening; he thought he was seeing a vision. ¹⁰ They passed the first and second guards and came to the iron gate leading to the city. It opened for them by itself, and they went through it. When they had walked the length of one street, suddenly the angel left him. ¹¹ Then Peter came to himself and said, "Now I know without a doubt that the Lord has sent his angel and rescued me from Herod's clutches and from everything the Jewish people were hoping would happen."

5 So Peter was kept in prison, but the church did what they were good at doing—earnestly praying to God for him. They realized it was humanly impossible to get Peter released. They knew that "the earnest prayer of a righteous man has great power and wonderful results" (James 5:16, TLB). We must never underestimate the effective power of a praying church.

6 The night before Herod was to bring him to trial, Peter was sleeping between two soldiers, bound with two chains, and sentries stood guard at the entrance. The execution date had been set and Peter was to die the following day. Peter was able to sleep soundly in spite of his circumstances because he trusted the Lord. He could later advise believers to "cast all your anxiety on him because he cares for you" (1 Peter 5:7). He was more than conqueror.

7 God is never late in delivering His people. His hand is not too short to help those who are in need. He sent an angel. Angels are ministering spirits who care for God's people (Hebrews 1:14). They are a higher order of creation than man. Suddenly an angel of the Lord appeared in Peter's cell and a light shone in the darkness. He struck Peter on the side and woke him up. "Quick, get up!" he said, and the chains fell off Peter's wrists. The guards were probably deep asleep and did not know what was going on.

8 The angel gave Peter some specific instructions in a businesslike manner. Then the angel said to him, "Put on your clothes and sandals." And Peter did so. "Wrap your cloak around you and follow me," the angel told him. The angel was on a rescue mission. The angel could do the extraordinary, but Peter must do the ordinary.

9 Peter followed the angel out of the prison, but he had no idea that what the angel was doing was really happening; he thought he was seeing a vision. Peter was naturally confused and did not understand what was going on. The whole experience was so amazing that Peter thought he was seeing a vision, like the one he had at Joppa (Acts 10:10).

10 They passed the first and second guards and then came to the iron gate leading to the city. It opened for them automatically by itself, and they went through it. When they had walked the length of one street, suddenly the angel left him. It took only one of God's secret agents to set Peter free. The angel's mission was completed. There was no farewell or further instructions. Peter could now fend for himself.

11 Then Peter came back to himself and said, "Now I know without a doubt that the Lord has sent his angel and rescued me from Herod's clutches and from everything the Jewish people were hoping would happen." He suddenly knew that his release from prison was real. Peter walked through the dark streets to where believers would likely gather. What happened next was one of the amusing moments in the Bible.

The Answer Kept Knocking

Verses 12-17: When this had dawned on him, he went to the house of Mary the mother of John, also called Mark, where many people had gathered and were praying. ¹³ Peter knocked at the outer entrance, and a servant named Rhoda came to answer the door. ¹⁴ When she recognized Peter's voice, she was so overjoyed she ran back without opening it and exclaimed, "Peter is at the door!" ¹⁵ "You're out of your mind," they told her. When she kept insisting that it was so, they said, "It must be his angel." ¹⁶ But Peter kept on knocking, and when they opened the door and saw him, they were astonished. ¹⁷ Peter motioned with his hand for them to be quiet and described how the Lord had brought him out of prison. "Tell James and the other brothers and sisters about this," he said, and then he left for another place.

12 When he realized that he had actually been released, he went to the house of Mary the mother of John, also called Mark, where many people had gathered and were praying. Back then there were no church buildings. Believers met from house to house. The house of Mary was a principal gathering center for believers in Jerusalem. Mary was the sister of Barnabas and the mother of John Mark, who is the author of the gospel that bears his name.

13 On arriving at Mary's house, Peter knocked at the outer entrance. A servant named Rhoda (meaning "rose") came to answer the door. Believers had gathered at Mary's house, having an all-night prayer (or vigil) for Peter's release from prison. It is ironic that the answer to their prayer was standing at the door, and yet they did not have enough faith to open the door for him.

14 When she recognized Peter's voice, she was excited and overjoyed. As a servant, Rhoda had to get permission from Mary to open the door for Peter. The best she could do was to share the news with those who were praying. So she ran back without opening it and exclaimed, "Peter is at the door!" But they would not believe her. They expected the worst and would not accept God's best.

15 "You're out of your mind," they told Rhoda. They believed that it was absolutely impossible for Peter to escape prison. But she was not easily intimidated. When she kept insisting that it was so, they said, "It must be his angel." This reflects their belief in guarding angels. But why would an angel knock the door? Their unbelief only led confusion. The conversation went back and forth while Peter was still standing at the door.

16 While all this argument and confusion was going on inside, Peter kept on knocking. It was time for them to stop praying and do something. When they finally opened the door and saw him, they were astonished. What was amazing was their slowness in trusting God for answered prayers. They were so joyful and excited that Peter had to calm them down.

17 Peter motioned with his hand for them to be quiet and described how the Lord had brought him out of prison. He told them how an angel helped him escape from prison. "Tell James and the other brothers and sisters about this," he said, and then he left for another place. He returned to Jerusalem later (Acts 15:7-11). Peter specifically wanted James to know about what had happened to him. By this time, James, the Lord's brother (not son of Zebedee), had become a leader in Jerusalem church.

NOTES

1. John MacArthur, *The MacArthur New Testament Commentary: Acts 1-12* (Chicago, IL: Moody Publishers, 1994), pp. 321,322.

Chapter 27

HEROD'S DEATH

Acts 12:18-25

Herod Executes the Guard

Verses 18,19a: In the morning, there was no small commotion among the soldiers as to what had become of Peter. ¹⁹ After Herod had a thorough search made for him and did not find him, he cross-examined the guards and ordered that they be executed.

18 In the morning, there was no small commotion among the soldiers as to what had become of Peter. Peter's mysterious disappearance caused an uproar among the soldiers who were responsible for watching him. The soldiers knew the repercussions of losing a prisoner. The Roman law required that guards serve the sentence or receive the same punishment the escaped prisoner should have received. They were in serious trouble. They had to report to Herod.

19a Herod made a thorough search for Peter. They made sure he was not hiding somewhere in the prison or in Jerusalem. When they did not find him, Herod cross-examined the guards and ordered that they be executed. Instead of killing Peter, Herod executed the guarding soldiers. Herod failed to learn from experience that he could not fight against God.

Herod's Presumption and Death

Verses 19b-23: Then Herod went from Judea to Caesarea and stayed there. ²⁰ He had been quarreling with the people of Tyre and Sidon; they now joined together and sought an audience with him. After securing the support of Blastus, a trusted personal servant of the king, they asked for peace, because they depended on the king's country for their food supply. ²¹ On the appointed day Herod, wearing his royal robes, sat on his throne and delivered a public address to the people. ²² They shouted, "This is the voice of a god, not of a man." ²³ Immediately, because Herod did not give praise to God, an angel of the Lord struck him down, and he was eaten by worms and died.

19b Then Herod Agrippa went from Judea to Caesarea and stayed there. Disgusted and frustrated, Herod turned his back to Judea and went to stay in Caesarea, a predominantly Gentile coastal city. Caesarea remained an insignificant city until Herod the Great, the grandfather of Herod Agrippa, developed it. Herod Agrippa remained there until he died.

20 Herod now diverted his attention to petty complaints from people in two cities. He had been quarreling with the people of Tyre and Sidon, which were coastal cities on the Mediterranean. They now joined together and sought an audience with him. After securing the support of Blastus, a trusted personal servant of the king, they asked for peace, because they depended on the king's country for their food supply. With such an economic dependence on Israel, it was important that the people of Tyre and Sidon make peace with Herod Agrippa.

21 On the appointed day, Blastus was to present the case of the settlement to Herod. Herod was to address the delegates from the two cities. He was to make a statement of reconciliation and cooperation. He wore his royal robes (made wholly of silver), sat on his throne, and delivered a public address to the people. We are told that a vast multitude gathered that day to hear Herod Agrippa.

22 The people were overwhelmed by Herod's great speech. They shouted, "This is the voice of a god, not of a man." The crowd attributed to him the honor of a god. Flattery and human praise could be dangerous. Herod did not rebuke them. He was enjoying the praises of the crowd. He would reap the reward of those who claim divine honors for themselves and usurp God's position.

23 Immediately, because Herod did not give praise to God, an angel of the Lord struck him down, and he was eaten by worms and died. The angelic beings carry out God's bidding. He instantly sends an angel to strike down the foolish, ego-driven man. God does not always punish sin immediately as He is slow to anger, but He did so in this case. Herod Agrippa had gone too far and had crossed the boundary line. God would not share His glory with anyone. He hates pride.

The Progress of the Church

Verses 24,25: But the word of God continued to spread and flourish. ²⁵ When Barnabas and Saul had finished their mission, they returned from Jerusalem, taking with them John, also called Mark.

24 In spite of Herod's persecution, the Word of God continued to spread and flourish. This progress report was given in contrast with Herod's humiliating death. The church Herod brutally tried to suppress was growing and expanding. "At the beginning of Acts 12, Herod seemed to be in control, and the church was losing the battle. But at the end of the chapter, Herod is dead and the church—very much alive—is growing rapidly!"[1]

25 When Barnabas and Saul had finished their mission of bringing famine relief, they returned from Jerusalem. They took with them John, also called Mark. Mark, the author of the second gospel, was the cousin of Barnabas (Colossians 4:10). Mark was raised by a godly mother named Mary; prayer meetings were held in her house. From the next chapter, the focus will be on the missionary efforts of Paul.

NOTES

1. Warren W. Wiersbe, *Be Dynamic: Acts 1-12* (Colorado Springs, CO: David C. Cook, 1987), p. 182.

SELECTED BIBLIOGRAPHY

Adeyemo, Tokunboh (ed.), *Africa Bible Commentary* (Nairobi, Kenya: WordAlive Publishers, 2006).

Arnold, Clinton E., *Acts* (Grand Rapids, MI: Zondervan, 2002).

Barton, B. Bruce et al., *Life Application Bible Commentary: Acts* (Carol Stream, IL: Tyndale House Publishers, 1999).

Boles, H. Leo, *Acts* (Nashville, TN: Gospel Advocate Co., 1989).

Carlsen, Derek, *Faith & Courage: Commentary on Acts* (Arlington Heights, IL: Christian Liberty Press, 2000).

Fernando, Ajith, *Acts: The NIV Application Commentary* (Grand Rapids, MI: Zondervan, 1998).

Ger, Steven, *The Book of Acts: Witnesses to the World* (Chattanooga, TN: AMG Publishers, 2004).

Horton, Stanley M., *Acts: a Logion Press Commentary* (Springfield, MO: Logion Press, 2001).

Hughes, R. Kent, *Acts: The Church Afire* (Wheaton, IL: Crossway, 1996).

Kwon, Yon Gyong (ed.), *A Commentary on Acts* (Minneapolis, MN: Fortress Press, 2015).

MacArthur, John, *The MacArthur New Testament Commentary: Acts 1-12* (Chicago, IL: Moody Publishers, 1994).

Marshall, I. Howard, *Acts: Tyndale New Testament Commentaries* (Downer Grove, IL: InterVarsity Press, 1980).

Milne, Bruce, *Acts: Witnesses to Him* (Fearn, Ross-shire, UK: Christian Focus Publications, 2010).

Ogilvie, Lloyd J., *Acts: The Communicator's Commentary* (Waco, TX: Word Books, 1983).

Phillips, John, *Exploring Acts* (Grand Rapids, MI: Kregel Publications, 1986).

Smith, Chuck, *The Book of Acts* (Costa Mesa, CA: The Word for Today, 2013).

Stott, John R. W., *The Message of Acts* (Downers Grove, IL: IVP Academic, 1990).

Thomas, Derek W. H., *Acts: Reformed Expository Commentary* (Phillipsburg, NJ: P&R Publishing Co., 2011).

Thompson, Richard P., *Acts: a Commentary in the Wesleyan Tradition* (Kansas City, KS: Beacon Hill Press, 2015).

Wagner, C. Peter, *The Book of Acts: a Commentary* (Ventura, CA: Regal From Gospel Light, 2008).

Wiersbe, Warren W., *Be Dynamic: Acts 1-12* (Colorado Springs, CO: David C. Cook, 1987).

Williams, David J., *Acts: Understanding the Bible Commentary Series* (Grand Rapids, MI: Baker Books, 1990).

Willimon, William H., *Acts: Interpretation* (Louisville, KT: WJK Press, 1988).

INDEX